JOHNNY'S READING SKILLS

A handy reference book for teachers, students, parents,
and others who are interested in reading development
and in reading improvement.

by

Edwin R. Rodgers

Reading and Study Skills Teacher
Bay Point Junior High School
St. Petersburg, Florida

Johnny Reads, Inc.
Educational Publisher
St. Petersburg, Florida

CONTENTS

Page

A Message from the Author   5
Let Johnny Speak for Himself   7

PART I

HELPS TO BETTER READING

Section 1   The Five Part Key That Opens the Door to Success. . . .   11
Section 2   This Is Very Important   12
Section 3   What Does a Sentence Tell Me?   13
Section 4   What's in a Paragraph?   15
Section 5   How Is a Lesson Organized?   19
Section 6   How Should I Study a Lesson?   24
                 Skim-Preview   24
                 Get Ready To Read; Question   25
                 Read; Self-Quiz and Recite; Review by
                 Rereading   26
                 Review by Retelling   28
Section 7   Step Up to Better Test Grades   31
                 Tests and Test Grades - An Introduction   32
                 Getting Ready for the Test.   33
                 Learning Hard-To-Remember Information   36
                         Some Types of Tricks.   37
                 Taking the Test   39
                         General Information   39
                         Essay Test   39
                         Objective Test.   44
                         Some Major Kinds of Objective Tests. . .   46
Section 8   How I Can Improve My Reading Comprehension.   48
                 Comprehension Skills   57
Section 9   How I Can Build a Bigger Reading Vocabulary   61
Section 10   What I Should Do about Reading Speed   66
Section 11   Skimming - What Is It?   75
Section 12   Skimming in Action   77
                 Skim-Preview a Lesson before Reading It   78
                 Skimming Helps Me Find Answers for Assigned
                 Questions   80
                 Skimming Helps Me Find Information for a
                 Report or for a Term Paper   85
                     Finding Information in Books   86
                     Finding Information in Magazines   89

(Continued)

(Contents, Continued)

PART II

WORD STUDY

		Page
Section 13	Alphabet, Consonants, Vowels	93
Section 14	Consonants	94
	Consonants and Their Sounds	95
	Consonants That Like To Be Different	96
	Some Consonants Blend	100
	Some Consonants Make Teams	102
	Some Consonants Are Silent Sometimes	104
Section 15	Vowels..................................	106
	Introduction to Vowels...................	107
	When Y Is a Vowel	110
	Long V̄owel Sounds....................	111
	When Should I Use a Long Vowel Sound?.	111
	Short Vowel Sounds	113
	When Should I Use a Short Vowel Sound?.	113
	Regular Exceptions to the Vowel Sound Clues ..	114
	Vowel Sound Teams and Vowel-Consonant Teams	117
	Major Teams...................	117
	Minor Teams...................	128
	Vowels in Unaccented Syllables............	131
	Summary of Vowel Sounds	133
Section 16	Freaks - More about Exceptions................	135
Section 17	Words and Parts of Words....................	138
	Compound Words	139
	Prefix, Root Word, Suffix................	140
	Let's Continue with Prefixes.........	141
	Let's Continue with Suffixes.........	149
	Root Words That Change	159
	More about Prefixes, Roots, and Suffixes	161
	Making English Words from Latin Roots.	161
	Making English Words from Greek Roots	164
	What Is a Syllable?....................	167
	How Can I Divide a Word into Syllables?	169
	Clues for Dividing a Word into Syllables.	170
	Accented Syllables and Unaccented Syllables...	174
	Patterns of Accent	177
	Clues for Accenting Syllables........	178
Section 18	What I Can Do To Figure Out a Word That I Don't Recognize	184
	Index	187

A MESSAGE FROM THE AUTHOR

The author hopes that this book will reach several different groups of people.

Primarily, this is a reading skills reference book to be used by teachers and students in connection with teaching and learning. The author hopes that this book will help to make the job of both a little easier.

Parents are becoming more and more interested in the work that their children are doing at school. The author believes that this could be a healthy trend and hopes that it continues in the right direction.

This book, then, is also for parents — to give them insight into the reading skills that we teachers are trying to get across to their children. It is possible, too, that those parents who gain an understanding of the reading skills might be able to reinforce at home what we teachers are trying to accomplish at school. This kind of partnership has great potential.

Adult education is a wonderful thing and fortunately is expanding rapidly. Many adults enroll in reading improvement classes, realizing how important it is to be a good reader; realizing, too, that a good reader can become an even better reader. Many adults, however, would like very much to attend a reading improvement class but are unable to do so for a variety of reasons. The author hopes that this book will help these people to accomplish their objectives at home.

More and more adults, other than teachers, parents, and adult students, are becoming increasingly interested in the subject of Reading and in the improvement of reading. They have read controversial articles on the subject in magazines and in newspapers and probably would like to be able to get more first-hand information. This book should help to enlighten these sincerely interested people.

There are a few people who seem to think of learning to read as being a simple task and of reading itself as being a simple skill. On the contrary, learning to read is not simple. Learning to be a good, independent reader might be as difficult for a youngster as it can be exciting and challenging. Nor is reading itself a simple skill. In fact, it is not a skill at all. Instead, actual reading is the end result of the inter-working of many skills, some of them quite complex.

So the author hopes that this book will reach these people, too. If it does, perhaps it will help to open their eyes and their minds. This, in turn, could result in a change of heart on their part, especially toward those children who are struggling, sometimes desperately, to learn how to read acceptably.

Finally, there are the critics. If they examine this book carefully, thoughtfully, and with an open mind, perhaps they will realize that we are teaching reading skills in the schools today.

The author wants to take this opportunity to express his appreciation to Mr. John W. W. Patrick, Principal of Bay Point Junior High School, St. Petersburg, Florida, for his constant interest in the improvement of reading and study skills. By creating a favorable atmosphere for reading and study skills instruction through his sincere interest in the program, and by providing ample class time for instruction, Mr. Patrick has contributed to the development of this book.

The author thanks Mrs. Cecil Stepp and Miss Anne Richmond for critically reading the manuscript of Johnny's Reading Skills. The author appreciates their criticisms and comments. Mrs. Stepp and Miss Richmond are members of the faculty of Bay Point Junior High School, St. Petersburg, Florida.

The author also wants to thank the many pupils in the many classes who, over a period of many years, have used the author's material. By doing so, they have helped to develop much of the content of this book as well as the form in which much of the content appears. Some of the pupils have been valuable and valued critics. The author appreciates their cooperation.

LET JOHNNY SPEAK FOR HIMSELF

Much has been written about Johnny during the past few years: about what Johnny can do and what he can't do — mostly the latter. His reading development (or the lack of it) seems to be an especially favorite football for the critics to kick around.

It seems to this teacher that Johnny should have a chance to defend himself and his record of progress. If Johnny were allowed to speak out for himself, he very likely might say something like this:

"My name is Johnny. A lot of people have been talking about me and writing about me. I think maybe it's time for me to say something for myself. So I've asked Mr. Rodgers to write down the information in this book for me, since he can write down stuff better than I can, 'cause he's a lot older than I am, I guess.

"This book will give you an idea of some of the things I've been learning about reading. It might surprise some of you grown-ups to find out there is so much a kid has to learn in order to be a really good reader. Were you taught these things when you were in school?

"This book will help me, too, and it will help a lot of other Johnnys, both boys and girls. 'Cause we forget things that we have learned, the same as you grown-ups do. But now, when we forget something that we have learned about reading, we can look it up in this book, and then we will know it again.

"When you grown-ups finish studying this book, I hope you will think better of us and about what we are learning in our reading classes."

This is Johnny's book. When you see the pronoun I, the I does not refer to Mr. Rodgers. The I is Johnny. And the I is the person who is using this book.

PART I

HELPS TO BETTER READING

SECTION 1

THE FIVE PART KEY THAT OPENS THE DOOR TO SUCCESS

1. I must have faith in myself; I must really believe that I can succeed.

2. I must really want to succeed.

3. I must be willing to work hard; I must be willing to do the things that will help me to succeed.

4. I must be patient; I must not get discouraged if progress seems to be slow. (I must realize that progress usually develops little by little. This is the way nature often works. Success in developing skills seldom is gained in a short time.)

5. I must learn to relax and not be tense and anxious and worried.

SECTION 2

THIS IS VERY IMPORTANT

This book has many helpful suggestions. It is good to know about them, but just knowing about them doesn't do much good. I need to use them over and over regularly. If I do, they will become habits, and I will do them without even thinking about them. Then they will really help me, and I will be a much better reader and a much better student.

SECTION 3

WHAT DOES A SENTENCE TELL ME?

Each sentence that I read tells me these two things:

1. <u>Who</u> or <u>what</u> I am reading about.

Jack hit the ball.   The ball went far away.

<u>Who</u> I am reading about.   <u>What</u> I am reading about.

2. <u>What</u> the person or thing did.

or

<u>What</u> happened to the person or thing.

Jack hit the ball.   Jack was hit by the ball.

<u>What</u> the person did.   <u>What</u> happened to the person.

The sentence might also tell me one or more of these things:

3. <u>When</u> it happened.

Jack hit the ball this afternoon.

<u>When</u> it happened.

4. <u>Where</u> it happened.

Jack hit the ball to left field this afternoon.

<u>Where</u> it happened.

5. <u>Why</u> it happened.

Jack hit the ball to left field this afternoon, because the left fielder was out of position, and Jack wanted a home run.

<u>Why</u> it happened.

6. <u>How</u> it happened.

Jack hit the ball very hard to left field this afternoon, because the left fielder was out of position, and Jack wanted a home run.

<u>How</u> it happened.

7. The sentence also might tell me <u>how</u> <u>much</u> or <u>how</u> <u>many</u>. For example:

Jack likes to play baseball a lot.

<u>How</u> <u>much</u>.

Jack hit two home runs last week.

<u>How</u> <u>many</u>.

We can see from the examples above that usually we get a meaning from a group of words working together — not from each word separately.

If I try to get the meaning of a sentence by thinking of each word separately, I'll have a hard time trying to under-stand what the sentence is supposed to tell me. Therefore, as I read a sentence, my mind should group together the words that work together to give the correct meaning of that part of the sentence.

SECTION 4

WHAT'S IN A PARAGRAPH?

A paragraph should have one main idea and some facts or details or bits of information that help to explain the main idea, or that help to support the main idea, or that help to prove the main idea, or that help to develop the main idea. Some of the information in the paragraph will be important information, while some of the information will not be very important.

When I study a paragraph, my first job will be to decide what is the main idea in the paragraph. If I have trouble doing that, I should ask myself a question like one of these: "What is this paragraph mostly about?" or "Why did the author write this paragraph?" or "What idea or thought is the author trying to get across to me in this paragraph?" or "The author wrote this paragraph mostly to tell me what?" or "The bits of information in this paragraph are working together to create what main idea or thought?" The answer to any of those questions will be the main idea of the paragraph.

The main idea of the paragraph might be stated as the "topic sentence" at the very beginning of the paragraph, at the very end of the paragraph, or somewhere in-between the first of the paragraph and the last of the paragraph. Sometimes, however, no sentence actually states the main idea. Then I must figure out what the main idea is and state it in my own words.

Next, I should decide what are the important bits of information in the paragraph — the ones that I need to remember. And what are the bits of information that are not important and that I do not need to make a special effort to remember? In making this decision, I need to keep in mind the main idea of the paragraph. This is necessary, because the paragraph's main idea is what determines whether information in the paragraph is important or not.

This sounds like a lot of work that will require a lot of time. But I should remember that this is a skill. And I should remember that any skill — a skill in passing a football, a skill in guarding my opponent in basketball, a skill in making a cake, a skill in using tools, a skill in reading — I should remember that any skill improves with practice. As

I use a skill again and again regularly, my ability to use that skill gets better and better. The more I use the skill, the sooner it will become a habit. Then I will be able to use the skill more smoothly, and I will be able to use the skill more quickly and at the same time more correctly.

Reminder to Teachers: Here are some of the main patterns that might be found in a paragraph:

1. topic sentence — expanding, explaining, discussing, and/or commenting — conclusion (or no conclusion)

A knowledge of study skills is very important. If you do not know the best ways to study, you will take longer to study than you should. A knowledge of study skills makes it easier for you to study a lesson. You will understand the lesson better, and you will remember the information longer.

2. key thought — repetition

Spring is a pleasant and a popular time of the year. Many people choose spring as their favorite season, because the weather is so pleasant then. If somebody asked, "When is the best time of the year?" lots of people would reply, "Spring." Fall is a nice season, too, but for a large number of people, spring is even nicer than fall.

3. cumulative details — climax

The temperature began to drop. Down, down, down it went. The air got colder and colder. The water in the lake got colder and colder. The water began to turn to ice. The ice got thicker and harder. At last we could go ice skating.

4. question — answer

Why should a person learn about study skills? There are too many reasons to put into one paragraph, but here are a few: Knowing about study skills will make it possible for a person to study a lesson better, faster, and more easily. He will get more information and ideas from a lesson, and he will be able to get the information and the ideas with less effort. He will have the information and the ideas better organized in his mind. That will help him to remember the information and the ideas longer.

5. problem — solution

While Jimmy was reading, he came to a word that he did not recognize. He tried to let the rest of the sentence and the sounds of the word help him to figure out the word. But that didn't work. He tried to divide the word into syllables and sound out the word. But the word still stumped him. Finally Jimmy got the dictionary and found out what the word sounded like.

6. question — question

Why are so many people moving to Florida? Is the weather a cause? Are people looking for an escape from severe winter temperatures? Are people tired of struggling with conditions caused by too much ice and snow? Are people looking for a more pleasant year-round way of life? Just what are the reasons?

7. facts — conclusion

When Bill has an assignment to study, he uses a quiet, comfortable place. He puts other thoughts out of his mind. He skim-previews the lesson before he starts to read it. He forms questions about each section of the lesson before he starts to read that section. When he reads, his mind is active and is thinking about what he is reading. From time to time he stops reading, and he recites — he quizzes himself about what he has just read. If necessary, he reviews (re-reads) that part. Bill knows how to study a lesson.

8. conclusion — facts or proof or evidence

Bill knows how to study a lesson. When he has an assignment to study, he uses a quiet, comfortable place. He puts other thoughts out of his mind. He skim-previews the lesson before he starts to read it. He forms questions about each section of the lesson before he starts to read that section. When he reads, his mind is active and is thinking about what he is reading. From time to time he stops reading, and he recites — he quizzes himself about what he has just read. If necessary, he reviews (rereads) that part.

9. opinion — reason

I think that spring is a nice time of the year. Spring weather usually is not too hot and is not too cold. After having to bother with heavy clothes during much of the winter, it is a relief not to have to wear coats, jackets, and sweaters. Now the flowers begin to grow again. Soon they will bloom and add beauty to yards, forests, and countrysides.

10. reason — opinion

Spring weather usually is not too hot and is not too cold. After having to bother with heavy clothes during much of the winter, it is a relief not to have to wear coats, jackets, and sweaters. Now the flowers begin to grow again. Soon they will bloom and add beauty to yards, forests, and country-sides. I think that spring is a nice time of the year.

11. detailed information (sometimes numbered)

There was very little grass in the yard. Weeds covered most of the yard, and they were about waist-tall. Sandspurs seemed to be everywhere. The old wooden fence needed paint. The house had a broken window at the front. Other than that, the outside of the house seemed to be all right.

12. series of incidents

The little girl toddled forward on uncertain legs. Suddenly she fell forward and sprawled on the ground. Her lips puckered, and for a few seconds she seemed to be ready to start crying. Then she saw her beloved teddy bear. Instead of crying, she squealed with delight. She started toward her trusted companion nearby, the world a happy place again.

SECTION 5

HOW IS A LESSON ORGANIZED?

(In this section, when we speak of a lesson, we mean a chapter in a textbook.)

It is a lot easier to do a job well if the work is organized and if I know how the work is organized.

Studying is an important job for people who are in school. Studying things like science or geography or history often seems to be a lot harder than it should be. That is true a lot of times because I don't know how the lesson is organized. I should know how the lesson is organized before I start to read it. Then I should use the outline of the lesson as I study. That will make it easier for me to study. That also will improve by ability to recognize and learn the important ideas and information in the lesson. Finally, that will help me to remember the important ideas and information.

A lesson like science or geography or history usually is organized like an outline, starting with the main title of the lesson:

I. Title of the lesson
   A. Subtitle for the first section of the lesson
      1. Main idea of the first paragraph in this section
         a. Information about the main idea in this paragraph
         b. Information about the main idea in this paragraph
         c. Information about the main idea in this paragraph
      2. Main idea of the second paragraph in this section
         a. Information about the main idea in this paragraph
         b. Information about the main idea in this paragraph
         c. Information about the main idea in this paragraph
      3. Main idea of the third paragraph in this section
         a. Information about the main idea in this paragraph

      b. Information about the main idea in this paragraph

      c. Information about the main idea in this paragraph

B. Subtitle for the second section of the lesson

    1. Main idea of the first paragraph in this section

      a. Information about the main idea in this paragraph

      b. Information about the main idea in this paragraph

      c. Information about the main idea in this paragraph

    2. Main idea of the second paragraph in this section

      a. Information about the main idea in this paragraph

      b. Information about the main idea in this paragraph

      c. Information about the main idea in this paragraph

    3. Main idea of the third paragraph in this section

      a. Information about the main idea in this paragraph

      b. Information about the main idea in this paragraph

      c. Information about the main idea in this paragraph

C. Subtitle for the third section of the lesson

    1. Main idea of the first paragraph in this section

      a. Information about the main idea in this paragraph

      b. Information about the main idea in this paragraph

      c. Information about the main idea in this paragraph

    2. Main idea of the second paragraph in this section

      a. Information about the main idea in this paragraph

      b. Information about the main idea in this paragraph

      c. Information about the main idea in this paragraph

    3. Main idea of the third paragraph in this section

      a. Information about the main idea in this para-

graph
b. Information about the main idea in this paragraph
c. Information about the main idea in this paragraph

(Of course, a lesson might have more than three sections, or it might have less than three sections. A section of the lesson might have more than three paragraphs, or it might have less than three paragraphs. A paragraph might have more than three important bits of information, or it might have less than three important bits of information. But the lesson still will be organized like an outline similar to the outline above.)

Now, the title of the lesson (I) tells me in a few words what the whole lesson is mostly about. In other words, the title of the lesson tells me or suggests to me the main idea of the whole lesson.

Each subtitle (A, B, C, etc.) tells me or suggests to me the main idea of that section of the lesson. So together the subtitles tell me or suggest to me how the author is going to develop the main idea of the whole lesson. In other words, each subtitle helps to tell me or helps to suggest to me the plan that the author will use to develop the main idea of the whole lesson. That is the way in which the subtitles are related to each other and to the lesson's main title.

Each paragraph has a main idea. The main idea of each paragraph tells something about the main idea of that section of the lesson. So together, the paragraphs' main ideas develop or explain the main idea of that section of the lesson. That is the way in which the main idea of each paragraph is related to the main idea of each other paragraph in that section of the lesson. That also is the way in which the main idea of each paragraph is related to the subtitle of that section and to the main title of the whole lesson.

Finally, in each paragraph there are important bits of information that work together to create the main idea of the paragraph.

Let's look at it another way:

information in a paragraph ⎫ information in a paragraph ⎬ information in a paragraph ⎭	Together they create the main idea of that paragraph.
main idea of a paragraph ⎫ main idea of a paragraph ⎬ main idea of a paragraph ⎭	Together they develop or explain the main idea of that section of the lesson (as suggested by the subtitle of that section of the lesson).
subtitle of a section of the lesson ⎫ subtitle of a section of the lesson ⎬ subtitle of a section of the lesson ⎭	Together they tell or suggest how the author is going to develop the main idea of the whole lesson (as suggested by the title of the whole lesson).

Now we'll show the lesson organization in the form of a diagram:

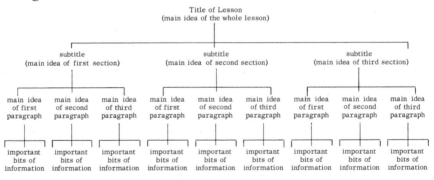

A lesson sometimes might start with a paragraph or with two or three paragraphs before I see the first subtitle. The purpose of that usually is to give me some general information about whatever the lesson will be about. It is like an introduction to the subject that is about to be discussed. This is important, because it helps to get my mind ready for the lesson.

A lesson sometimes might end with a paragraph or with two or three paragraphs called a summary. That section of the lesson might have the word Summary as a subtitle. The summary is not a regular part of the lesson organization, but it is very important, anyway. In the summary, the author is stating what he thinks are the most important things that have been discussed in the lesson.

Reminder to teachers: As you know, all books do not stick strictly to the above organizational pattern. There might be variations. For example, each section might be further divided into smaller sections, each with its own subtitle, and each of these smaller sections might be even further subdivided into still smaller sections, each with its own subtitle. Corresponding sections can be identified readily by the size or by the type of the subtitles.

The organizational pattern that we have presented in detail may be regarded as a basic pattern which can be expanded easily to fit the exact organizational pattern of any textbook.

SECTION 6

HOW SHOULD I STUDY A LESSON?

Skim-Preview

Before I start to read the lesson, I should skim-preview the lesson. I should start with the title of the lesson. That tells me or suggests to me the main idea of the whole lesson. The main title tells me or suggests to me what the whole lesson mostly is about. So I read the title, and I think about what it says and about what it means.

Next, I should skim through the lesson, looking for, reading, and thinking about each subtitle in the lesson. That will show me how the lesson is organized. It will show me the pattern or plan that the author used when he wrote the lesson. It will give me a bird's-eye view of the lesson. It will show me how the different parts of the lesson are related to one another. Those subtitles will tell me or suggest to me how the main idea of the whole lesson will be created or developed. At this point in my study, I might well ask myself this question: How will the ideas contained in or suggested by those subtitles work together to develop the idea or meaning that the bigger title suggests? While I skim-preview a lesson, I also should notice illustrations. I should think briefly about how the illustration fits into that section of the lesson and how it will help me to understand that section of the lesson better.

Why is it important for me to do those things? Here is the reason: Ideas and information that are not related to one another are much harder to understand, learn, and remember. Ideas and information that are related to one another are much easier to understand, learn, and remember.

Suppose I start to read a lesson without skim-previewing it first. My mind has no idea how the lesson is organized. So my mind has no idea how the different parts of the lesson are related to one another. This is the hard way to study a lesson, because I am trying to make my mind read, understand, learn, and remember ideas and bits of information without having the slightest idea of how they fit into the overall picture — the lesson as a whole. That is like trying to work a jigsaw puzzle without knowing what the picture as a whole is like.

But suppose I do skim-preview the lesson before I start to read it. This is like looking at the picture of the jigsaw puzzle before I start to work the puzzle. The Skim-Preview helps me to get a general idea of what the lesson is about. Before I start to read the lesson, I already know how the lesson is organized. I know what the most important ideas of the lesson are. I know in a general way how the different parts of the lesson are related to one another. Now as I read ideas and bits of information, they will have more meaning to me, because I can see how they fit into the overall pattern of the lesson. Now I can see how the ideas and bits of information are related to one another. So now they make sense. And now it is much easier for me to read, understand, learn, and remember the ideas and the bits of information.

This is a lot like taking a trip by car. A person could just start on the trip and hope that he keeps on the right road. It's a lot better, though, to look over a road map first. Then the driver has a better and a clearer idea of what the trip will be like. He knows what roads he will be using and what places he will be traveling through. He now has the overall plan of the trip organized in his mind. This way, he can drive more confidently, he has less danger of getting lost, and he will get a lot more out of the trip.

The Skim-Preview also helps me to develop some interest in and curiosity about the lesson. We will discuss why that is so very important when we discuss "Get Ready To Read; Question".

(See also "Skimming in Action": "Skim-Preview a Lesson before Reading It" on pages 78-79.)

Get Ready to Read; Question

Now I return to the first subtitle. But I am not ready to start reading that section yet. First I should read the subtitle again. If there are illustrations like pictures, maps, charts, graphs, diagrams, or tables, I should notice them again and read the captions carefully. Then I will be ready to refer to them when they are mentioned in the section that I am getting ready to read.

Once again I return to the subtitle and read it. I am impressing upon my mind what the main idea of this section will be. Now I should change the subtitle into a question, using words like who? what? when? where? why? how? how much? how many? For example, the subtitle might be "Long Vowel Sounds." It could be changed to "What are long vowel sounds?" Also I should ask myself questions like these: What will be the main idea in each paragraph in this section? How will those main ideas work together to develop or explain the idea that the subtitle suggests? What will be the important bits of information in each paragraph?

Why is that questioning important? This is why: The mind does not soak up ideas and information like a sponge. Instead, the mind must be active. It must reach out and look for the ideas and the information. The questioning helps my mind to be alert, awake, active. The questioning makes my mind reach out and look for ideas and for information as it actively looks for answers to questions.

Also, I know very well that it is hard to understand and learn something if I am not curious about it and if I am not interested in it. On the other hand, I know very well that I can understand and learn something faster and easier if I am curious about it and if I am interested in it.

The questioning, then, also is intended to help me develop some genuine curiosity about and interest in the section of the lesson that I am about to read. The curiosity and the interest will make it easier for me to understand and learn the ideas and the information that I am reading about. The curiosity and the interest will help me to remember the ideas and the information, too.

Read; Self-Quiz and Recite; Review by Rereading

Next, I start to read the section.

First, I should read the section once fairly quickly. The purpose is to get a general, overall picture of the ideas and the information in that section. This is like a movie camera that is recording a scene from a distance. The camera is getting a picture of a large area, but it is not picking up the details of any one part of the scene.

Now I return to the beginning of that section and read carefully. This is like the movie camera moving closer to the scene. Now the camera is recording only a part of the large scene at a time, but I can see this part of the picture much more clearly and in much greater detail than I could see the large scene.

As I read each paragraph, I look for the information in the paragraph. I think about how the various bits of information work together to create the main idea of that paragraph. In this way I will be able to decide what the main idea of the paragraph is. After I find out what the main idea of the paragraph is, I will be able to tell what are the important bits of information in the paragraph. That is true because the process works two ways: The bits of information create the main idea; the main idea, in turn, determines what the important bits of information really are. (This is discussed more fully in Section 4, "What's in a Paragraph?" on pages 15-18.)

I also think about how the main idea of that paragraph relates to the main idea of each other paragraph in that section. That is, I think about how together those main ideas develop or explain the idea or meaning that the subtitle of that section of the lesson suggests.

As I read, I should use the suggestions discussed in Section 8, "How I Can Improve My Reading Comprehension". Especially important at this time are suggestions 5, 7, 8, 9, 10, 11, and 12 on pages 52, 53-56.

Notice that from time to time I stop reading and I quiz myself on what I have just finished reading. I self-quiz and recite.

The Self-Quiz and Recite step is very important. In fact, it probably is just about as important as the actual reading of the lesson. That is true because if I don't have this self-quiz, the time that I used to read the lesson will have been partly wasted. That is a rather startling statement, but it also is a true statement. The reasons that the statement is true are discussed in Section 8, "How I Can Improve My Reading Comprehension," suggestion number 11 on pages 55-56. Right now I should turn back to that suggestion and read it carefully again.

Notice that the Self-Quiz and Recite step is followed immediately by a rereading review of the part of the lesson covered by the self-quiz if the self-quiz indicates that a rereading review is needed. The reasons that this is so very important also are discussed in Section 8, suggestion number 11.

Review by Retelling

Now I have finished reading the whole lesson. Is there anything else for me to do before I put away the book? You bet there is! I should go back to the beginning of the lesson. Then section by section I should retell myself the main ideas, how they are related to one another, and how they are related to their important bits of information. If I don't do this, I am likely to forget more than I should. If I forget too much, I will have wasted a lot of the time that I spent studying and learning the main ideas and the important information. But if I do review by retelling them right now, I will be getting them better organized in my mind. I will be getting them fixed more clearly and more strongly in my mind. That will help me to remember them better and longer.

If possible, I should review by retelling the lesson to myself again the next day sometime before the class starts. This is important because a person forgets a lot during the twenty-four hours that follow the original study of the lesson. This second Review by Retelling will help me to recover what I have forgotten. It also will greatly strengthen the important ideas and information in my mind. That will reduce considerably the amount that I will forget.

So I see that studying a lesson is not just reading the lesson. Reading the lesson certainly is very important, but it is just one of the important parts of studying a lesson.

If I really study a lesson, I will do each of these:

1. I will Skim-Preview.
2. I will Get Ready To Read; Question.
3. I will Read.
4. I will Self-Quiz and Recite.
5. I will Review by Rereading (if necessary).
6. I will Review by Retelling.

Here, now, is a summary, giving some of the main ideas and information that we have been discussing:

The Skim-Preview is intended to help me in several ways. It should help me to develop some curiosity about and interest in the lesson. The Skim-Preview should help me to get a general idea of what the lesson is about. The Skim-

Preview also should help me to see and to understand the overall organization of the lesson. This is important, because it will help me to notice and to understand the relationships between and among the different parts of the lesson, between and among the main ideas of the lesson, and between and among the important bits of information and the main ideas of the lesson.

The Get Ready To Read; Question is intended to help me develop some curiosity about and interest in the lesson. One good way to make up a question for a section of the lesson is to turn the subtitle into a question. These are some of the words that can help me to do that: who? what? when? where? why? how? how much? how many? I also should alert my mind to be looking for the main idea and the important information in each paragraph. That includes understanding how the ideas and the information are related to each other and understanding how they are related to ideas and information in other paragraphs.

The Skim-Preview and the Get Ready To Read; Question make it possible for me to study more quickly. They make it easier for me to find the main ideas and the important bits of information in the lesson. They also help to make the ideas and the information stick in my mind.

First I will Read a section (the paragraphs that are under a subtitle) fairly fast, just to get a general picture of what the main ideas and the information are like. Then I will read the section carefully, so that I can learn and remember the main ideas and the important information. I will use the suggestions in Section 8 of this book — especially suggestions 5, 7, 8, 9, 10, 11, and 12.

The amount that a person will read before stopping to go over what he has read will vary. The least amount probably will be one paragraph. The largest amount probably will be one section. The amount depends on how well a person can understand and remember what he reads.

The Self-Quiz and Recite step really has two main purposes. First, it lets me know whether or not I understand and remember the main ideas and the important bits of information. Second, it strengthens my understanding and my memory of the main ideas and the important bits of information. That will help me to remember longer and will help to cut down on how much I forget.

If the Self-Quiz and Recite indicates that I have only a fuzzy or a hazy idea of what I have read, then I should Review by Rereading immediately. I should have the main idea or ideas and the important bits of information clearly organized and fixed in my mind before I leave that part of the lesson. The Review by Rereading will help me to remember what I have read. The Review by Rereading will help to keep me from forgetting so much of what I have read.

The Review by Retelling comes right after I have finished reading all of the lesson. The Review by Retelling helps to get the many important ideas and the many important bits of information organized and fixed more clearly and strongly in my mind. That will help to keep me from forgetting them.

If possible, I also should Review by Retelling the lesson again the next day before class. That will help me to recover what I have forgotten since my original study of the lesson.

If this study system (or any other study system) is really going to help me to become a better student, I must use it over and over regularly until it becomes a habit. Then I will use the system without even realizing that I am using it. Then it really and truly will help me.

SECTION 7
STEP UP TO BETTER TEST GRADES

Tests and Test Grades — An Introduction

Getting Ready for the Test

Learning Hard-To-Remember Information
    Some Types of Tricks

Taking the Test
    General Information
    Essay Test
    Objective Test
    Some Major Kinds of Objective Tests

TESTS AND TEST GRADES - AN INTRODUCTION

The main purpose in getting ready for a test and taking a test is not to get a good grade. The main purpose is to be sure that I understand, know, and remember the important ideas and the important information that I have been studying, and to get the ideas and the information well organized in my mind.

Getting ready for a test should help me to strengthen my understanding and knowledge of the important ideas and the important information, should help me to get them better organized in my mind, and should help me to remember them better. Then the test should find out whether or not I do understand and know the important ideas and the important information, whether or not I do have them well organized in my mind, and whether or not I do remember them. If I do, I probably will get a good grade. If I don't, my grade probably will be sort of sad-looking.

The grade, then, is not important by itself. It is important, though. The grade is important, because it is supposed to represent how well I know, understand, and remember the things that I have been studying, and how well I have them organized in my mind. So it is perfectly natural that most of us want to get good test grades.

How does a person go about getting good test grades?

There are right ways to do a thing, and there are wrong ways to do the same thing. If we use a wrong way, we probably won't be very successful. But if we use a right way, there is a much better chance for success. This is true with most of the things that we must do in life. It also is true with getting ready for tests and with taking tests.

First, we shall examine some of the things that we should do to get ready for a test. Then we shall examine some of the things that will help us to do a good job when we take the test.

(When we use the word test, we are thinking mainly of a test that covers a considerable amount of material — such as a chapter test, a unit test, a six-week test, or a semester test. However, many of the suggestions also will help us to get ready for and take smaller tests and quizzes.)

GETTING READY FOR THE TEST

1. A wise student starts to get ready for a test before the test even is announced. He does that by studying, understanding, and organizing his daily assignments day by day. In other words, he "keeps up" with his daily assignments; he does not let himself fall behind in his work.

If I am wise, that is one of the things that I will be sure to do.

2. When a test is announced, I will set up a study schedule for the test, and I will use the schedule. The schedule will make me start studying for the test several days before the test.

3. I will do my best to keep in good mental and physical health. This means that I must get enough sleep (that is especially necessary the night before the test), I must get some recreation and some physical exercise every day, and I must eat well and sensibly.

4. When I am supposed to be studying, I will study; I will not waste time.

5. I will start in my book with the first page that the test will cover. I will go through the pages one section (the paragraphs that are under a subtitle) at a time. I will Review by Retelling each section (see "Review by Retelling" in Section 6, pages 28, 30); I will reread the section if necessary; I also will be sure that I remember important information in illustrations like charts, diagrams, graphs, pictures, etc. Then I will go on to the next section.

6. I will get a clean sheet of notebook paper. This will be a "Test Reminders Paper". As I review each section, I will make a written note of anything important that I think I might forget (for example: 1. See page 248, paragraph 4: facts about types of transportation in Parkonia). This will keep me from overlooking things that I should review more than once. It also will save me a lot of time, since I know exactly where to find the information that I need to review again. This timesaving will be especially important the last time that I review just before the test.

If a fact or some information is hard to remember, I also should do this: I should put a note in the margin of the paper to review the fact or the information for a few minutes each day (See "Learning Hard-To-Remember Information" on pages 36-37).

7. If I have class notes or study notes, I will be sure to review them as I review the corresponding sections of the book.

8. If I outlined each lesson carefully when I first studied it, or if I took careful notes when I first studied each lesson, I can use them instead of the book as my main study material. Then I will need to use the book only to double-check my outline or my notes if I am doubtful about something.

9. I will think about what the teacher has emphasized. I will be sure that I understand and know those things thoroughly. I might be able to guess what some of the test questions will be.

10. The night before the test: By this time I should have finished reviewing everything for the test at least once. So tonight I will spend a short time (probably no more than an hour) reviewing for the test — I will review only the things that I might forget, and things that might give me trouble if they are on the test (things that I have listed on my "Test Reminders Paper"). I will go to bed early and get a good night's sleep.

11. The day of the test: Using my "Test Reminders Paper", I will take a few minutes to go over the main points and things that might need a quick, last minute refresher.

12. I will be sure that I have all of the materials that I will need for the test.

13. A few minutes before the class starts: I will go to the restroom.
While I am in the restroom, I also will do this: I will run cold water over my hands and wrists. I will put cold water on my elbows (back and front of each elbow). I will

put cold water on my face, temples, forehead, head (a girl probably will not want to put water on her head, but there is no reason why a boy should object), and on the back of my head and neck.

14. I will go to class on time or a little bit ahead of time. I will get settled at my desk, get my test-taking materials ready, and make myself as comfortable as possible.

15. I will not let myself be worried, scared, or anxious. I will not let myself be all tight inside. Those feelings will not help me at all. Instead, they will hurt me. They will keep me from doing my best. They will keep my mind from thinking clearly and accurately.

So I will be as calm as possible, I will be as relaxed as possible, and I will be confident (but not overconfident). Why? Because I know that I have been using my time wisely. I know that I have done my best to get ready for the test.

LEARNING HARD-TO-REMEMBER INFORMATION

Suppose that I have trouble remembering an important fact or some important information. Here is what I can do:

1. I will read the information carefully.

2. If I am reviewing for a test, I will make a special marginal note about the information on my "Test Reminders Paper".

3. I will think about the information until I understand it.

4. I will understand why the information is important; I will understand how the information fits into the lesson.

5. I will work up some interest in and curiosity about the information.

6. I will try to get my mind to make a picture of the information (see Section 8, "How I Can Improve My Reading Comprehension," suggestion 9, on pages 53-54).

7. I will try to get my mind to connect the information with something that I already know about or with something that I like (see Section 8, suggestion 10, on pages 54-55).

8. I will say the information out loud.

9. I will write the information.

10. I will talk about the information with other people.

11. If I can use the information in any other helpful way, I will do so.

12. I will review the information for a few minutes every day.

13. If I am reviewing for a test: Three days before the test:

a. If I still am having trouble making the information stick in my mind, I will start spending more time each day going over the information.

b. If necessary, I also will figure out some trick to help fix the information in my mind. This trick will help me to remember the information. From now until the test I will use the trick every time I review that information.

(I can use that trick idea when I am studying a daily assignment, too. But I should not use tricks unless it is necessary to do so.)

Some Types of Tricks

1. I can make up a catchy word:
The information that I need to remember: The best months for the experiment are April, May, and June.
Making a catchy word: I can take the first letter of the name of each month (A, M, J), switch the letters around, and make the catchy word jam. It is easy to remember jam. Then on the recitation or on the test, I will think of the name of each of the three months that come together and that begin with the letters JAM.
The catchy word does not have to be a real word. It can be a made-up word.

2. I can make up a formula:
The information that I need to remember: There are five parts to the answer. I keep forgetting how many parts the answer has. When I remember that there are five parts, I usually remember what each part is.
A possible formula: I want the right answer. There are five fingers on my right hand. So each finger on my right hand will represent one part of the answer.

3. I can make up a jingle:
The information that I need to remember: World War II ended in 1945.
A possible jingle: Nineteen hundred forty-five
Saw World War II's peace arrive.

4. I can make up a sentence:

The information that I need to remember: Six of the most important city areas in Florida are Jacksonville, Miami, Pensacola, St. Petersburg, Tallahassee, and Tampa.

Making a sentence: I can use the first letter in each name. I can let each letter begin a word that will help to make a sentence. (In this particular sentence, I will keep the name St. Petersburg). Here is the sentence: My pop took Jack to St. Petersburg.

It will be easier to remember a sentence, where together the words mean something than it will be to remember a list of names if those names don't especially mean anything to me. Then later, the sentence will help me to remember the names of the cities.

TAKING THE TEST

General Information

1. I will be as calm as possible. I will be as relaxed as possible. I will be confident (but not overconfident).

2. I will begin working as soon as the teacher is ready for me to start.

3. I will read and clearly understand the directions before I start to answer any question.

4. I will do exactly what the directions tell me to do.

5. I will keep my mind on answering the questions.

6. When I get my corrected test paper back from the teacher, I will be sure that I understand why my wrong answers are wrong.

Essay Test

1. I will read all of the questions before I start to answer any question.

2. I will decide about how much time I should spend on each question. If I don't do that, I might run out of time before I finish the test.

3. I will reread each question carefully before I begin to answer it. I will be sure that I understand clearly and exactly what the question is asking me or what it is telling me to do.

4. A lot of times it helps to use scratch paper. Then I can jot down ideas and facts that otherwise might slip my mind. Also, I might be able to use the scratch paper to organize my ideas and information before I start to write the answer to a question. (Before I use scratch paper, I must be sure that the teacher approves. If the teacher seems not to like the idea, I should ask him if he will initial or put his name at the top of a blank piece of paper and let me use just

that piece of paper for scratch paper.)

5. I should answer first the questions that I know the answers for, but which I think that I might forget if I answer other questions first. (I will be sure to leave enough space on my answer papers for answers to questions that I am skipping temporarily.)

6. Next, I should answer the questions that I know the answers for and which I think that I will not forget.

7. I should leave for last the questions that I am not sure about. In order to answer those questions, I probably will have to do some mental digging. I probably will have to dig back into my mind and try to uncover the answers for them. I will have to do a lot of careful thinking. That might take some time, but I should not get jittery. Often I will be able to find in my memory the information that I need, if I think carefully and calmly, and if I relax. I must not let myself get nervous or worried or scared.

8. Before I start to write the answer to a question, I should do this: I should get the ideas and information for the answer organized in my mind. I should be sure that I know what I am going to write before I start to write my answer. I should use my scratch paper if that will help and if the teacher has approved.

9. I will be sure to include in my answer all of the information that is needed to answer the question, but I will leave out information that does not help to answer the question.

10. Here are some of the main types of essay questions with information about how to answer them. If I use these suggestions, my answer should have the kind of information that the question is asking for:

a. The question asks or tells me to compare two or more things. I will be sure that I tell how the things are alike and how they are different.

b. The question asks or tells me to contrast two or

more things. I will be sure that I tell how they are different.

   c.   The question asks or tells me to <u>define</u> something. I will be sure that I write a definition of the thing.
After I tell what the thing means, I should do this: I should
give an example of what I mean, if I can think of a good
example.

   d.   The question asks or tells me to <u>describe</u> something. I will be sure that I tell clearly and accurately what
the thing is like. I will tell about the thing, I will give an
account of it, I will give a word picture of it.

   e.   The question asks or tells me to <u>discuss</u> something. That question is asking for a lot of information. I
will be sure to write all that I know about the thing. This
answer will include the other types of answers (such as
comparing, defining, describing, explaining, etc.).

   f.   The question asks or tells me to <u>explain</u> something. Depending on how the question is worded, I will be
sure to do one or more of these: 1) write how to do it or
how it was done or how it happened; 2) write why it happened, why it should happen, why it was done in a certain
way, or why it should be done in a certain way (that is, give
the reasons); 3) make clear and plain whatever it is that
needs explaining; 4) write what the thing means; 5) try to
bring out an understanding of the thing.

   g.   The question asks or tells me to <u>illustrate</u> something. First I will determine whether the question is calling
for a drawing or for a word answer. If a word answer is
needed, I will be sure that my answer makes the thing or
the meaning of the thing clear by giving a good, clear example of the thing.

   h.   The question asks or tells me to <u>list</u> some
things. I will write a list of those things (1, 2, 3, etc., one
right after the other or one right under the other). I will not
have to describe them, explain them, or discuss them in any
way (unless the question actually says to describe, etc., in
addition to making a list). I just have to make the list.

i.   The question asks or tells me to <u>outline</u> something. I will write a general account of the thing, giving only the main information about the thing. (The question or the teacher should also say whether to write the information in outline form or in regular sentences and paragraphs.)

j.   The question asks or tells me to <u>sketch</u> something. First I will determine whether the question is calling for a rough drawing or for a word answer. If a word answer is needed, I will write briefly, giving only the main information about the thing.

k.   The question asks or tells me to <u>summarize</u> something or to write a <u>summary</u> of something. I will write as briefly as possible all of the main information about the thing.

l.   The question wants to know <u>who</u>. . . . I will be sure to name the people or the person that the question is asking about.

m.   The question wants to know <u>what</u>. . . . I will be sure to write about the things or about the actions that the question is asking about.

n.   The question wants to know <u>when</u>. . . . I will be sure that my answer gives the time (such as a date) that the question is asking about.

o.   The question wants to know <u>where</u>. . . . I will be sure that I tell where — I will be sure to write the location or the place that the question is asking about.

p.   The question wants to know <u>why</u>. . . . A "why" question is asking for a cause or a reason or for causes or reasons, so I will be sure that my answer has the cause or the reason or the causes or the reasons that the question is asking about. A "why" question wants a "because" kind of answer.

q.   The question wants to know <u>how</u>. . . . I will be sure that my answer tells how — my answer will tell the way something is done, was done, will be done, or should be done.

Or a "how" question might want to know the way some-thing is, the way it was, the way it will be, or the way it should be. If that is the way the question is worded, then my answer will tell the way something is, the way it was, the way it will be, or the way it should be. For example: <u>How</u> is the weather in that country? ➡ The weather is <u>warm</u>.

Or a "how" question might mean "in what way". For ex-ample, the question, "<u>How</u> does skimming help a student?" means "<u>In what way</u> does skimming help a student?"

Or a "how" question might be like a "why" question. That is, the "how" question might be asking for a cause or a reason or for causes or reasons. For example, the question, "<u>How is it that</u> good reading ability is so important for suc-cess in school?" really wants to know, "<u>Why</u> is good reading ability so important for success in school?" or "<u>What are</u> the <u>**reasons**</u> that good reading ability is so important for success in school?" or "What **causes** good reading ability to be so important for success in school?"

Or a "how" question might be the same as a "how much" or a "how many" question. For example, "<u>How</u> long did the war last?" means "<u>How many</u> years (or months, etc.) did the war last?"

r. The question wants to know <u>how much</u> or <u>how many</u>. . . . I will be sure that my answer <u>gives</u> the <u>number</u> or the quantity that the question is asking about.

11. Sometimes I might write in my answer all of the in-formation that I can think of at the time, but I might feel or think that I have left out some important information. In a case like that, if I just can't seem to remember the rest of the information, I should do this: I should leave on the paper enough space to finish the answer. Then I should go on to the next question that I plan to answer. Later, I will go back to the "unfinished" answer, if I still have enough time.

12. I will write as clearly as I can. My teacher will ap-preciate that. Writing clearly might help my grade, too, be-cause a teacher can't give me credit for an answer that he can't read.

13. I will use correct English (capitalization, punctua-

tion, spelling, subject-predicate agreement, etc.)

14. I will reread my answer before I go on to the next question that I plan to answer.

15. I have finished answering all of the questions. I will look over all of my answer pages before I hand in the paper. Doing that is important so that I will be sure I have done everything that I am supposed to do.

(For simplicity, we have used the word question to refer to a test item whether it is in the form of a statement or of a question.)

Objective Test

1. I will read the whole question carefully. I will be sure that I understand the question before I try to answer it.

2. If a question "stumps" me — if I am not sure what the correct answer is — I will put a pencil mark by the number of the question. I will go on to the next question and to the other questions that follow. If I have time when I get to the end of the test, I will go back and try to figure out the answer to each question that I skipped the time before.

3. I will glance at the clock from time to time to be sure that I am not working too slowly or too fast.

4. I am working on a classification test question. I should read the whole list carefully before I start to mark my answer. Also, before I start to mark my answer, I must figure out what classification the question wants me to think about.

5. I am working on a classification test question. Sometimes it is easier to work this correctly if I put a check mark by each part that belongs in the same classification.

6. I am working a completion test question. Before I

write my answer, I must be sure that I understand what the sentence means. My answer must make sense when it is used in the sentence.

7. I am working on a <u>matching</u> test question. I should read both lists carefully before I start to mark my answers.

8. I am working on a <u>matching</u> test question. It is easier to work that correctly if I put a check mark by each of the pair as the two are matched.

9. I am working a <u>multiple-choice</u> kind of question. I will read carefully and understand clearly all of the possible answers before I choose the answer that I think is the correct answer.

10. Sometimes on a <u>multiple-choice</u> question, I will find that all of the answers except two are no good. But both of the two seem to be correct. In a case like that, I must be extra sure that I know exactly what the question asks; I must be extra sure that I know exactly what each of the two answers means. Often there will be just a slight difference between the two, so I must use clear, thoughtful, careful thinking in order to select the right one.

11. I am working on a <u>rearrangement</u> test question. I should read the whole list carefully before I start to mark my answers.

12. I am working on a <u>rearrangement</u> test question. It is easier to work that correctly if I put a check mark by each part as I use it.

13. I am taking a <u>true-false</u> test. I do not know the answer to a question and have been unable to figure out what the answer should be. I am going to guess the answer. The question has a main word like <u>all</u>, <u>always</u>, <u>everything</u>, <u>none</u>, <u>never</u>, or <u>nothing</u>. For such a question, an answer of "false" or "no" is a safer guess than is an answer of "true" or "yes". That is not always true, of course, but it usually is true. For example: **All** people are honest. Unfortunately, that is a false statement.
If that word (<u>all</u>, <u>never</u>, etc.) is qualified, there is a

better chance that the statement is true than if the word is not qualified. For example: a) There **always** is a breeze blowing at the beach. b) There **almost always** is a breeze blowing at the beach. The second statement has a better chance of being true than the first statement has. If I do not know the answer — if I have to guess — I should guess false for a statement worded like a, and I should guess true for a statement worded like b. I probably would not always be right, but I probably would be right more often than I would be wrong.

14. I am working on a true-false question. Part of it seems to be true, but part of it seems to be false. If part of a true-false question is false, I should mark that question false. The statement as a whole must be true in order for the question to be answered true.

15. Suppose the answers are marked on a separate answer sheet. Then any marks that I have to make on the question paper I should make only with a pencil, and I should make them as light as possible. When I no longer need to use the marks, I should erase them carefully.

16. Now I have finished the test. Before I hand in my paper, I should look over the test paper and my answer paper to be sure that I have done everything that I am supposed to do.

(For simplicity, we have used the word question to refer to a test item whether it is in the form of a statement or of a question.)

Some Major Kinds of Objective Tests

1. Classification
   Example: Which of these things should not be in this list?

a. orange	d. lemon
b. grapefruit	e. apple
c. lime	f. tangerine

2. Completion
   Example: The capital of Newfoundland, Canada, is ____ .

3. Matching
   Example: Match an English word with a Spanish word
            that means the same. There is one extra
            Spanish word.
   1. man   a. pluma
   2. ink   b. casa
   3. pen   c. hombre
   4. house   d. poco
                            e. tinta

4. Multiple Choice
   Example: The port of Charleston is in what state?
      a. Georgia   c. South Carolina
      b. North Carolina   d. Virginia

5. Rearrangement
   Example: These men became President of the United
            States from 1901 to 1961. List them in the
            order in which they served as President.
      a. Calvin Coolidge   f. Franklin D. Roosevelt
      b. Dwight D. Eisenhower   g. Theodore Roosevelt
      c. Warren G. Harding   h. William Howard Taft
      d. Herbert Hoover   i. Harry S. Truman
      e. John F. Kennedy   j. Woodrow Wilson

6. True-False (This kind of test might be answered by
               true or false, by T or F, by yes or no, by
               + or -, by + or 0, or in some other similar
               way. Usually the test directions will tell
               which kind of answer to use.)
   Example: Answer "yes" if the statement is correct;
            answer "no" if the statement is not correct.
      1. Portland, Oregon, is located on two sides of the
         Willamette River.
      2. Houma, Louisiana, is the parish seat of Terre-
         bonne Parish.
      3. The first capital of the United States of America
         was Washington, D. C.

SECTION 8

HOW I CAN IMPROVE
MY READING COMPREHENSION

Comprehension means understanding. If I comprehend how to play basketball, I understand how to play basketball. If I comprehend how to fix a machine, I understand how to fix a machine. If I comprehend what I read, I understand what I read. Then I am reading with comprehension or with understanding.

If I don't comprehend or understand what I read, I am not really reading. I am just looking at words. In order to be really reading, I must be getting meaning from those words. I must comprehend or understand what those words are trying to tell me.

This section of Johnny's Reading Skills will tell me how I can improve my ability to comprehend or understand what I read.

1. If I really want to improve my reading comprehension, I must also improve my vocabulary. I must be able to recognize more words, and I must be able to recognize harder words. I also must know what those words mean.

If I try to improve my reading comprehension without doing those things, that would be like a carpenter trying to build a house without some of his important tools.

2. Punctuation marks are like road signs by the side of a highway. If the driver of a car ignores the road signs, he could get into serious trouble. If I ignore punctuation marks when I am reading, I could get into serious trouble, too. I might think that the sentence means one thing, but the sentence might not mean that at all. The sentence might mean something very different from what I thought it meant.

Let's see how a change in punctuation completely changes the meaning of this sentence:

John, our friend is here.
John, our friend, is here.

In the first sentence, somebody is talking to John. The person is telling John that their friend is here. The sentence doesn't tell me the name of the friend.

In the second sentence, I don't know the name of the

person that somebody is talking to. This sentence does tell me the name of the friend. The friend's name is <u>John</u>, and the sentence tells me that John is here.

So in my English class, I should try my best to understand what the punctuation marks are supposed to tell me. I must know that before I can read with clear understanding.

3. Very often a word is used instead of a word that already has been used in the sentence or in the paragraph. Sometimes two or three words are used that way. This is done to keep from having to repeat the same word or words. Using those substitute words (like pronouns) makes reading more interesting.

If I am going to understand clearly what such a sentence is trying to tell me, I must know what the substitute word refers to or what word it is taking the place of.

Here are examples of what I am talking about:

a. Bill put his book on the table so <u>he</u> would know where to find <u>it</u>. (he = Bill; it = his book)

b. Our team is called "Falcons". We think <u>the name</u> is a good <u>one</u>. (the name = Falcons; one = name)

c. Some athletes practice a lot. <u>Such athletes</u> usually become very good players. (Such <u>athletes</u> = athletes who practice a lot)

d. Oranges are grown in different parts of the world. <u>Many</u> are squeezed to make a delicious drink. (Many = many <u>oranges</u>)

e. You should spend your vacation in Costa Rica. The people <u>there</u> are very nice, and the scenery is beautiful. (there = in <u>Costa</u> Rica)

f. There are so many vegetables in Dale's garden. He has <u>more</u> than <u>he</u> can use. (He = Dale; more = more <u>vegetables</u>; he = Da<u>le</u>)

g. Jack wants to visit Florida during the winter. Many people visit Florida <u>at this time of the year</u>. (at this time of the year = during <u>the winter</u>)

h. Sue cannot go to the game this week, but she might be able to do so next week. (to do so = to go to the game)

Many words are used like the underlined words in the sentences above. I must be on the look-out for such a word, and I must be sure that I know what it means in that sentence. Doing this will help me to understand more clearly what I am reading about.

4. Conjunctions are connecting words. They are used often to connect one part of a sentence with another part of the sentence. They are important to know about, because they show how the meaning of one part of a sentence is related to the meaning of another part of the sentence.

A conjunction, then, is a very useful clue that will help me to understand clearly what the sentence is trying to tell me.

The conjunctions in the sentences below show how one action is related to the other action so far as the time of happening is concerned.

a. He laughed as he sat down.   (He laughed and sat down at the same time.)

b. He laughed while he sat down.   (He laughed and sat down at the same time.)

c. He laughed before he sat down.   (He laughed first; he sat down last.)

d. He laughed after he sat down.   (He sat down first; he laughed last.)

e. As he sat down, he laughed.   (Same as a.)

f. While he sat down, he laughed.   (Same as b.)

g. Before he sat down, he laughed.   (Same as c.)

h. After he sat down, he laughed.   (Same as d.)

The conjunctions in the sentences below show how the meaning of one part of the sentence is related to the meaning of another part of the sentence:

    i.   We went on a picnic, and we had a good time.
(and tells me this: What happens in the second part of the sentence is what we would expect after reading the first part of the sentence.)

    j.   We went on a picnic, but we did not have a good time.
(but tells me this: What happens in the second part of the sentence is not what we would expect after reading the first part of the sentence. Other conjunctions that will give this meaning are however, still, yet. Nevertheless might also be used to give this meaning.)

    k.   We started the game, although it was raining.
(although tells me this: The first part of the sentence is true in spite of what the second part of the sentence says. Another conjunction that will give this meaning is though.)

    l.   He makes good grades, because he knows how to study.
(because tells me this: The first part of the sentence makes a statement. The second part of the sentence gives the reason why the first part of the sentence is true or possible. Other conjunctions that will give this meaning are for, since. Since also is used as a conjunction in another way: We have not heard from them since they went away. In a sentence like that, since means: What is stated in the first part of the sentence began when the second part of the sentence happened.)

    m.   He knows how to study, so he makes good grades.
(so tells me this: The first part of the sentence gives the reason why the second part of the sentence is true or possible. Consequently, therefore, thus might also be used to give this meaning.)

    n.   We have a better chance to succeed if everybody works together.
(if tells me this: The last part of the sentence tells what needs to happen in order for the first part of the

sentence to happen. Another conjunction that will give this meaning is _provided_. _If_ also is used as a conjunction in another way: I wonder _if_ she heard the bell. In a sentence like that, _if_ means: The last part of the sentence will finish the thought that started in the first part of the sentence.)

o. We might get lost _unless_ we follow the directions carefully.

(_unless_ tells me this: The first part of the sentence will happen if the last part of the sentence does not happen. Or we can express this same meaning another way: The second part of the sentence needs to happen in order to keep the first part of the sentence from happening.)

Those are some of the conjunctions. I need to understand how they work. Then it will be easier for me to learn how other conjunctions work.

I need to know how conjunctions work in order to understand clearly what many sentences are trying to tell me.

Now I am getting ready to read. I might be reading for pleasure, or I might be reading a lesson assignment. The rest of these suggestions tell me what I should do in order to get the most out of what I read.

5. I should forget everything around me. I should clear all other thoughts out of my mind. I should fix my complete attention on what I am reading. I should concentrate on what I am reading.

6. Before I start to read, I should look over the story or book or lesson to get an idea of what it is about. If there are illustrations like charts, diagrams, graphs, pictures, etc., I should look at them, too. I should read and think about the title and the subtitles.

If I am going to read for pleasure, I should now ask myself something like this: "I wonder what this chapter will be about?" or "I wonder what's going to happen in this chapter?" or "I wonder if that's a good title for this chapter?" or I could turn the title into a question with the help of a word like who? what? when? where? why? how? how much? how many?

If I am going to read a lesson assignment, I should do what was explained in Section 6, "How Should I Study a Lesson?": "Skim-Preview" and "Get Ready to Read; Question" on pages 24-26, 28-29.

Doing those things before I start to read will help to "warm up" my mind and get it ready to do a really good job of reading and studying.

Reminder to teachers: This is mental warming-up, similar to the physical warming-up before an athletic contest. It gets the brain ready for the mental requirements to follow. It gives the brain a preview of what is to be expected of it — a preview of the nature of the ideas and the information that it will be expected to look for, organize, understand, record (mentally or on paper), react to, and retain. It sets a purpose for the reading that is to follow, so the brain will have an objective instead of just working aimlessly. It attempts to make the reading-studying process less passive and more active.

7. When I start to read, my mind should be active and alert. My mind should be reaching out and looking for answers to the questions that I have in my mind or that I wrote down on a piece of paper before I started to read. My mind should be reaching out and looking for other related ideas and information, too.

As I read, I should think about what I am reading. I must not just look at the words or just say the words to myself. But I must think about what those words are telling me.

Reminder to teachers: Reading depends on thinking. Unless thinking is focused on the reading matter, there is no reading.

8. I must not try to get the meaning of a sentence word by word. Instead of trying to think of each word separately, I should do this: As I read a sentence, my mind should group together the words that work together to give the correct meaning of that part of the sentence. (See Section 3, "What Does a Sentence Tell Me?" on pages 13-14.)

9. I should try to get a picture in my mind of the things that I am reading about. In my mind, I should try to see clearly what is happening. In my mind, I should hear the

sounds. In my mind, I should smell the things that are being smelled or the important things that can be smelled. In my mind, I should feel the things that are being felt or the important things that can be felt. In my mind, I should taste the things that are being tasted or the important things that can be tasted.

Reminder to teachers: What we are trying to accomplish by suggestion 9 is sensory imagery. Well developed sensory imagery will help to make the student's reading more vivid, more life-like, and more alive than would be possible otherwise.

This skill can be applied to fiction-type reading and to study-reading in all subject areas. For example, in mathematics, the student can visualize the situation involved in a problem. In science, the student can picture in his mind the steps of an experiment and perhaps sense the odors involved. In geography, the student can picture in his mind the appearance of a region that is being discussed, and he can mentally react to or sense the sounds and the smells of the place. In literature, descriptions will become much more than words — the setting will come alive in the mind of the student.

We have mentioned only a few ways in which this important reading skill can be put to profitable use. The application of this skill is almost limitless in each subject area.

10. As I read, my mind should connect the ideas and the information I am reading about with ideas and information that I already have in my mind. That is, my mind should connect the new ideas and information with things that I already know about.

It is so much easier for my mind to take in new thoughts if those new thoughts can be related in some way to familiar old thoughts.

Here are some examples of what I mean:

I am studying about a jet engine. I know very little about a jet engine, but I can use what I have heard about jets and jet engines to help me with that lesson. I can look for ways that prove that my present knowledge is right or wrong or partly both. I can look for the reasons why my present knowledge is right or wrong or partly both.

If I know something about a gasoline engine, I can think about how the jet engine I am studying about is like a gasoline engine and how the jet engine is different from a gasoline engine.

Suppose I know nothing at all about a jet engine or any other kind of engine. There will be ways in which the jet engine works like things I do know about. These other things might have nothing to do with engines. That doesn't matter. What does matter is that I know about these things, and in some way they are like a jet engine. If I will hook these thoughts together in my mind, it will be much easier for me to learn about the jet engine.

Now I am studying my geography lesson. It is about Hawaii. Suppose that I have never been to Hawaii and really know nothing about the place. But I do know a lot about the place where I live. I also know about other places — places that I have visited and places that I have read a lot about. So as I study about Hawaii, I should think how it is like the places I know about, and how it is different from the places I know about.

This is sort of like going fishing. I am taking knowledge that is already in my mind, and I am using this old knowledge like I would use a baited fish hook. I am using this old knowledge to hook onto the new things that I am reading about. In this way I am fishing for, hooking, and pulling into my mind lots of new and important knowledge.

11. I am reading to get ideas and information (like a study assignment). I should stop from time to time and ask myself questions about what I have been reading. I should ask myself questions like these: "What is the main idea of this paragraph?" and "Why is that the main idea of this paragraph?" and "How is the main idea of this paragraph related to the main ideas of other paragraphs in this section of the lesson?" and "How is the main idea of this paragraph related to the main idea suggested by the subtitle of this section of the lesson?" and "What are the important bits of information in this paragraph?" and "Why are they important bits of information?" Sometimes it might be helpful for me to use questioning words like who? what? when? where? why? how? how much? how many? when I quiz myself (notice that the sample questions above made use of some of these questioning words).

What I am doing here is having a self-quiz or a little recitation with myself. Suppose I find that I can't answer the questions very well. Or suppose I find that I have only a hazy idea about what I have been reading. What should I do about it? Well, this is just plain common sense: If I don't know now the ideas and the information that I have just finished reading about, I surely won't know about them tomorrow in class. The sensible thing for me to do is to go back and reread (review) that part until it is clearly fixed in my mind.

Doing those things will help my mind to organize the main ideas and the important bits of information. That will help me to understand them better and will help to fix them more securely in my mind. So doing those things will help me to understand and to remember what I have read and studied. That will make it possible for me to cut down on how much I forget.

Reminder to teachers: Unless the student already finds it easy to get, understand, and retain the main ideas and the important bits of information, we suggest that at first he should stop after each paragraph and have his self-recitation. If necessary, he should reread the paragraph right then until he knows what it contains. Then he can go on to the second paragraph, and so on. With sufficient practice and mental training, the student later might be able to take two paragraphs at a time. If he becomes proficient in coping with this unit, he can start including three paragraphs at a time. In this way, many students eventually might be able to tackle a whole section at a time.

12. I am reading fiction, or I am reading non-fiction that is written like fiction. As soon as possible, I should pick out a character that I like. In my mind, I should let myself become that character while I am reading. And while I am reading, I should mentally live the experiences that the character has.

Reminder to teachers: If the student is experienced in the use of suggestion 9, he should be able to use suggestion 12 easily.

13. Suppose I come across something that I don't under-

stand. I try my best to figure it out, but I just can't seem to be able to figure it out. I am completely stumped. What should I do now? I should ask somebody who knows about such things. But I should not ask that person to tell me the answer. Instead, I should ask that person to help me figure it out.

If the other person just told me the answer, I would lose the mental practice that I probably need. And the next time something like that stumped me, I would have to ask for help again. I probably would forget the answer in a little while, too, if somebody just told me the answer.

But if the person helped me to figure it out for myself, that is much better for me. This way, my mind is getting good practice and training. If I come across something like that again, the next time I probably will be able to figure it out by myself. Also, if I figure out something for myself, I probably will remember it longer, even if somebody helped me.

Reminder to teachers: For maximum carry-over or transfer of learning from the reading class to the various content areas, these suggestions should be stressed repeatedly by the reading teacher and by the content area teachers in connection with the work in each content area. If this is done consistently, there should be good carry-over to the study-reading of those subjects. On the other hand, if direct application of these suggestions is not made systematically by the content area teachers, there might be very little transfer of learning from the reading class to the other areas of study.

That is true not only of the suggestions discussed in this section. It is equally true of information and of suggestions in any section of this book, if the information or the suggestions of that section can be used in connection with the work of some class.

Comprehension Skills

These are important comprehension skills that help to make me a good reader:

58

1. I can understand phrase and sentence meaning.

2. I can use punctuation marks as an aid to understanding what I am reading.

3. I can tell what pronouns (and other substitute words) refer to.

4. I can recognize key words in what I am reading.

5. I can notice and understand shades of meanings of words.

6. I can form and experience sensory images and impressions as I read. (That is, as I read, my mind and my imagination will help me to see, smell, taste, hear, and feel what is happening in the book, story, article, or lesson that I am reading.)

7. I can understand figurative language. (For example: **Exaggeration**: He jumped a mile high; **Simile**: She was gentle as a little lamb; **Metaphor**: She was a little lamb; **Personification**: The statue smiled its thanks to the friendly crowd.)

8. I can notice and recall important details or facts or bits of information. I can tell the important facts from the less important facts.

9. I can tell the main idea or central thought of a paragraph.

10. I can select and organize the details that support, prove, develop, or explain the main idea of a paragraph.

11. I can recognize and understand paragraph patterns.

12. I can understand and I can follow written directions.

13. I can understand comparisons that are made in whatever it is that I am reading. If what I am reading does not actually make comparisons but comparisons are needed, I can make the needed comparisons.

14. I can understand place and space relationships.

15. I can understand size relationships.

16. I can understand time relationships.

17. I can understand part-whole relationships.

18. I can understand cause and effect relationships.

19. I can understand the sequence of events or of ideas or of information. (This includes chronological order.)

20. I can identify myself with a character in fiction and in fiction-like material. That is, in my imagination, I can put myself in that person's place.

21. I can recognize and understand the emotional reactions of the people that I am reading about.

22. I can notice, understand, and evaluate character traits.

23. I can recognize and understand the problem and the plot in fiction and in fiction-like material.

24. I can recognize and understand the author's mood or tone, and in my imagination I can feel the mood of a selection or of a part of a selection.

25. I can recognize or I can figure out and I can understand the author's purpose, plan, and point of view.

26. I can interpret or explain the author's meanings. In order to be able to do that, I must be able to understand what the author actually says. I must also be able to figure out and understand what the author implies (the implications) — that is, what the author is suggesting or hinting without actually coming right out and saying so. (When I figure that out, I am making an inference. This also is called "reading between the lines".)

27. I can understand, appreciate, and enjoy different

types of humor.

28. I can usually predict the outcome of what I am reading.

29. I can tell the main idea or central thought of whatever it is that I am reading.

30. I can summarize what I read.

31. I can outline what I read.

32. I can take notes on what I read.

33. I can classify ideas and information.

34. I can recognize and understand the difference between emotive and informative writing.

35. I can take the ideas and the information that I am reading about and relate them to ideas and to information that I already have gotten by reading, by experience, and by observation.

36. I can read and think critically. This includes the ability to tell the difference between a fact and an opinion; the ability to evaluate the facts and the opinions; the ability to evaluate the source of the facts and of the opinions; the ability to compare and to evaluate different points of view, including the facts and the opinions involved and their sources; the ability to make inferences (see item 26 above); the ability to accept, to reject, or to withhold possible acceptance or rejection of a fact or of an opinion until I am able to get more information or until I have had enough time to evaluate the facts and the opinions (including their sources) further; and finally, the ability to form my own valid conclusions or generalizations.

37. I cannot remember everything that I read. So I figure out what the important things are, and I try to remember them.

SECTION 9

HOW I CAN BUILD
A BIGGER READING VOCABULARY

My listening vocabulary is made up of the words I understand when I hear somebody else talking. I know what those words mean when I hear them used. I started to build my hearing vocabulary when I was a tiny baby.

My speaking vocabulary is made up of words that I can use correctly when I talk. I know what those words mean, and I can use them to express my thoughts to others in conversation. I started to build my speaking vocabulary when I was able to say my first real word and knew what that word meant.

My reading vocabulary is made up of words that I know when I see them in writing. I can recognize those words correctly when I see them, and I know what those words mean. I started to build my reading vocabulary when I first recognized a word and knew what that word meant.

Finally, there is my writing vocabulary. My writing vocabulary is made up of the words I can use correctly when I am expressing my thoughts in writing. I began to build my writing vocabulary when I first wrote a word and knew what that word meant.

In this section of Johnny's Reading Skills, we are concerned mostly with the reading vocabulary. The suggestions below will tell me how I can build and develop my reading vocabulary.

I need to build a bigger vocabulary. That is true because a bigger vocabulary will make it possible for me to read, understand, and enjoy a lot more things than I can now.

1. I should listen for words that are new to me when other people are talking. When I hear a new word, I should make an effort to remember how the word was used. The first chance I get, I should think about that word. I should try to figure out what the word must look like in order to sound the way it does. I also should think about how the

word was used. Then I should try to figure out what the word must mean when it is used that way. Next, I should check the dictionary to see if the word looks like I figured it would look. I also should check the dictionary to find out if the word can mean what I thought it might mean.

I can add a lot of useful words to my vocabulary this way.

2. I am reading. Here is a word that I don't know. I can't figure out what the word is or what it means. Perhaps I can figure out what it sounds like, if it is a word that I've heard. But whether I can figure out what the word sounds like or not, I still can't figure out what the word means. What should I do?

What I should do depends on how important the word is right now.

If I need to know what the word means in order to know what the sentence and the paragraph are trying to tell me, I should look up the word in the dictionary right away.

But if I can get the meaning of the sentence and paragraph without that word, I should just quickly write down the word now. I will look it up in the dictionary later, when I get to a good place to stop reading.

Here is the reason for this suggestion: When I am reading, the important thing is to get the meaning of what I read — to get the main ideas and the important bits of information, and to know and understand how they are related.

Now, suppose I take time out from my reading to look up a word in the dictionary. That interruption breaks into the chain of ideas and information that I am getting from the reading. Therefore, I am putting a weak link into the chain of meaning that I am getting from the reading. It just isn't worthwhile to do that for a word that I don't need right now.

I should look up the word in a dictionary, yes, because many times in the future I probably will need to know the word. But right now is not the time to go to the dictionary for that word.

So I should not ignore words that stump me. I should not just pass over a word that gives me trouble. Either right now or a little bit later I should find out for sure what the word sounds like and what it means. In that way I constantly will be building up my vocabulary. And I will be increasing my ability to read, understand, and enjoy harder stories, articles, books, and lessons.

3. Many times I can figure out what a word means without having to look up the word in a dictionary. I can do that by the way the word is used in the sentence. Or there might be meaning clues in the sentence or in other sentences. Sometimes an illustration like a picture or a diagram might suggest what the word means.

Let's imagine that I am reading. As I read, I see the word <u>ageratum</u>. We'll pretend that I don't know what that word means. Let's consider these sentences and notice how they tell me what <u>ageratum</u> means:

a. Ageratum is a plant that has pretty flowers.
(The sentence comes right out and tells me what the word means.)

b. I saw some ageratum today. This is a plant that has pretty flowers.
(Some other sentence comes right out and tells me what the word means.)

c. I want to plant ageratum in my flower garden.
(The meaning of the sentence tells me about what the word means, though not as clearly as the other sample sentences do.)

d. I saw some ageratum today. This plant surely does have pretty flowers.
(The two sentences together tell me what the word means without coming right out and saying so. The sentences tell me indirectly what the word means.)

e. I saw some ageratum, a plant with pretty flowers. Or: I saw some ageratum, a plant with pretty flowers, while I was walking home.
(I notice that there is a comma right after <u>ageratum</u>. I also notice that the words right after the comma are telling me what <u>ageratum</u> means.)

4. Here is a sentence that doesn't make sense. I should not just ignore that sentence, because it might be an impor-

tant sentence in the paragraph. I should find out why the sentence doesn't make sense, and I should make the sentence make sense.

This is one reason why a sentence doesn't make sense: I think that I know what a certain word sounds like or what it means, but I am wrong. The word is not the word that I think it is.

So by making that sentence make sense, I add another word to my reading vocabulary.

5. I should read a lot, and I should read different kinds of stories, articles, and books (athletics, biography, travel, science, etc.). That will help me to add a lot of different kinds of words to my reading vocabulary.

6. I should be sure to use the information that is in the Word Study part of this book. If I forget some of that information, I should review it. The information about prefixes, roots, and suffixes will be especially helpful in figuring out the meaning of a word.

7. Perhaps there are word study charts in the room at school. Those charts might be on the wall or they might be on a stand. I should use those charts if I have trouble figuring out what a word sounds like.

8. I should remember that many words have more than one meaning. The meaning that the word has depends on what the whole sentence is trying to tell me.

Here are examples of what I am talking about:

a. 1. He saw a friend.
   2. He has a saw.
   3. He will saw the board.

b. 1. He bit the meat.
   2. He has a bit of meat.
   3. He took the bit from the tool box.

c. 1. The general is a stern man.
   2. The admiral is in the stern of the ship.

9. I should think about words.

I should think about what words look like and why they look the way they do.

I should think about what words sound like and why they sound the way they do.

I should think about what words mean, and I should think about how to use a word in order to make that word have a certain meaning.

10. I should have a notebook for words that give me trouble. I can call that notebook my "Review Words Notebook".

If I have trouble recognizing a word, I should find out what the word sounds like. Then I should write the word in my "Review Words Notebook".

If I am not sure what a word means, I should find out what the word means. (If the word was used in a sentence and if the word has more than one meaning, I should be sure that I find out what the word means in that sentence.) Next, I should think about the meaning of the word. Now I should make up three sentences of my own, using the word. Then I should ask somebody who knows about words to check my sentences. This is necessary and important in order to be sure that I used the word correctly. I now should write the word, meaning, and sentences in my "Review Words Notebook". Next comes the final step, and this is so very important: I should use that word when I am talking and when I am writing every time I have a chance to do so.

If I don't do those things, I probably will forget the word and its meaning pretty fast. Then the next time I come across the word, I will have to take the time and the effort to learn the word all over again.

If I do those things, they will help to fix the word and its meaning clearly and strongly in my mind. That will help me to remember the word and its meaning. Whenever I come across the word again, I will know what the word is and what it means. So doing those things saves me a lot of time in the long run. It also helps me to build a bigger reading vocabulary.

SECTION 10

WHAT I SHOULD DO ABOUT READING SPEED

Here is the important question that I must get answered about reading speed: When should I read more slowly, and when should I read faster? That is so very important, because fast reading is good only if I understand what I am reading fast. Understanding what I read is the most important thing. If I can read fast and understand what I am reading, that is good. But if I read fast and don't understand what I am reading, that is not good. Because speed by itself is not good. In order to be good, reading speed and reading understanding must go together, hand in hand.

This section of Johnny's Reading Skills will answer that question for me (that is, "When should I read more slowly, and when should I read faster?"). In this section of the book, I will find out when to change my reading speed. I will discover when I should read slowly and carefully and when I can and should read faster.

This section of the book also will tell me how I can improve or increase all of my reading speeds — my slow speeds, my fast speeds, and my in-between speeds.

We will start by answering that important question: When should I read more slowly, and when should I read faster?

1. A good automobile driver is not a one speed driver. He changes his speed. Sometimes he drives slowly. Other times he drives much faster. But at all times he uses a speed that is a good, safe speed for the situation that he is in at that particular time.

If I am going to be a good reader, I must be like a good car driver. I, too, must use different speeds when I read. I must match my reading speed with the reading situation that I find myself in at a particular time. I must not be a one speed reader.

These three things tell me whether to read slower or faster:

a. Suppose the car driver comes to a street where children are riding bicycles. Also, a lot of little children are playing by the side of the street. Any instant, one of them might dash out onto the street in front of the car. This is a hard driving situation, and a good driver is going to slow down his driving speed. He is going to drive slowly.

I am reading. I come to a place where many words are not familiar to me. I have to figure them out in order to understand what I am reading. Or perhaps there are ideas that are strange to me, and I have to figure out what in the world the author is talking about. This is a hard reading situation, and a good reader is going to slow down his reading speed. He is going to read slowly.

Let's go back to the car driver. The street that he's been driving slowly on now becomes a good highway. He has left the place where there were bicycles and where little children were playing. There is nothing in his way, and there is nothing that might suddenly get in his way. This is an easy driving situation. Within reason, a good car driver can safely increase his driving speed. Now he can and should drive faster.

The book that I've been reading now becomes easier to read. I've left the place where there were several words that I didn't know or where there were strange ideas that I had to figure out. Now, I know all of the words or almost all of them. The ideas are familiar to me, too. So there is nothing to get in the way of my understanding what I am reading. This is an easy reading situation. Within reason, a good reader can increase his reading speed. Now he can and should read faster.

This, then, is one thing that helps to tell me whether I should slow down my reading speed or whether I should speed up my reading speed: Is what I am reading hard or is what I am reading easy?

If I am reading something hard, I should read more slowly. But if I am reading something easy, I can and should read faster.

The easier the thing is that I am reading, the faster I should be able to read it with good understanding. If I read hard things and easy things at the same speed, I need a lot of practice. I need to practice slowing down for hard reading and speeding up for easy reading.

b. The car driver is driving in a place where he has never been before. He is not sure whether the traffic lights are at the side of the street or above the center of the intersection. He is not sure which streets are one-way streets. He is not sure exactly how to get where he wants to go. In other words, he is not familiar with this place where he is driving. A good car driver is going to drive more slowly when he is not familiar with the place where he's driving.

But the same car driver is now driving in a place that he knows about. He knows where the traffic lights are located. He knows which streets are one-way streets. He knows where to turn in order to get where he wants to go. He is familiar with this place. So within reason and within the speed limits, the car driver can safely drive faster.

The same is true about reading. There are some things that I know very little about. But there are some things that I know a lot about. If I am not familiar with the subject that I'm reading about, I'd better slow down. But if I am familiar with the subject that I'm reading about, I can and should read faster.

Here is an example of what I mean: Suppose I am reading about space travel. If I don't know much about space travel, I need to read more slowly. But if I already know a lot about space travel, I can and should read faster.

This, then, is another thing that helps to tell me whether I should slow down my reading speed or whether I should speed up my reading speed: How much do I already know about the subject that I am reading about?

If I am not familiar with the kind of material that I am reading, I should slow down my reading speed. But if I am familiar with the kind of material that I am reading, I can and should read faster.

c. Here is our car driver again. As he drives, he wants to be able to see something of the scenery. He wants to learn something about the places along the highway. He wants to find out some facts and bits of information about them. He wants to be able to remember as much as he can about the places he is driving through. He cannot do that and drive fast. To drive fast would be dangerous. Also, if he drives fast, he would not have time to take in all the facts and information that he needs.

So the driver keeps in the slow lane of the highway, and he drives as slowly as he needs to drive so that he
can accomplish his purpose safely.

At times he sees some detail in the scenery that
he needs more time to consider. So he pulls completely off
the highway to a parking place. There he stops so that he
will have time to think about what he sees and to get that
detail clearly fixed in his mind.

But suppose our car driver doesn't especially
care whether he finds out facts and bits of information about
the scenery or whether he doesn't. He just wants to get general ideas (ideas without details) in his mind about the
places he drives through. If he remembers any facts or bits
of information, okay. If he doesn't remember any facts or
bits of information, still okay. It's all the same to him. Just
those general ideas (those ideas without details) — that's all
he wants or needs. This time, the car driver can drive
much faster.

So it is with me when I read. This time I am supposed to learn and remember what I am reading about. I
need to look for, find, understand, organize, and remember
facts and bits of information. I cannot do that and read fast.
If I read fast, I will not have time to look for, find, understand, organize, and remember all of the facts and bits of
information that I need to get from what I am reading.

So I slow down my reading speed. I need to read
more slowly now. I need to read more slowly in order to
give my mind time to look for, find, understand, organize,
and remember facts and bits of information.

At times I will come across some fact or bit of
information or some thought that I need more time to consider. So I stop reading completely. Now I will have enough
time to think about that fact or that bit of information or that
thought, and I will have time to get it clearly fixed in my
mind. When I have done that, I can return to my reading.

But suppose I am reading just for pleasure, or I
am reading just to get general ideas (ideas without details)
in my mind of what happened. If I remember facts or bits
of information, okay. If I don't remember any facts or bits

of information, still okay. It's all the same to me. Just those general ideas (those ideas without details) of what happened — that's all I need to get from what I am reading. This time I can and should read much faster and still do what I am supposed to do.

This, then, is another thing that helps to tell me whether I should slow down my reading speed or whether I should speed up my reading speed: What is my purpose in reading this material? Why am I reading this material?

If I am reading to look for, find, understand, organize, and remember facts and bits of information, I should slow down my reading speed. But if I am reading for pleasure or just to get general ideas (ideas without details) of what happened, I can and should read faster.

Here is a summary of what we have been talking about:

Three things together tell me whether to slow down my reading speed or whether to read faster. These three things are:

a. Am I reading something hard, or am I reading something easy?

b. How much do I already know about the kind of thing that I am reading about?

c. Why am I reading it? What is my purpose for reading it?

Here is a chart-type summary of what we have been talking about:

		Slower Reading	Faster Reading
a. How hard is it?	it's hard:	✓	
	it's easy:		✓
b. How much do I already know about the subject?	not much:	✓	
	a lot:		✓
c. Why am I reading it?	for facts, details, information:	✓	
	for pleasure; for general ideas:		✓

Reminder: Be sure that you understand this, because it is very important: A person's reading speeds are an individual sort of thing. That is, a reading speed that is slow for you might seem awfully fast to another person. It might be the other way, too: A reading speed that is fast for you might seem awfully slow to somebody else. So when we say to read something fast, we mean that you should use your fast speed. When we say that you should read something slowly, we mean that you should use your slow speed.

Suggestion 1 told me that I should read some things slower and some things faster.

The rest of these suggestions will tell me how I can read faster than I can read now. I still will change my reading speed as Suggestion 1 said I should. But I will be making my slowest speed go faster than it is now. I will be making my fastest speed go faster than it is now. And I will be making all of my in-between speeds go faster than they go now.

That might not be easy, especially if I am the kind of person who hates to change his way of doing things. But I can make those changes if I really want to and if I practice regularly.

A person's reading speed is like a pair of shoes. I am used to my old shoes. They feel so comfortable, and I feel so at ease in them. I am used to my old reading speeds, too. They feel so comfortable, and I feel so at ease with them.

Now, new shoes often feel uncomfortable at first. I don't feel a bit at ease when I first use them. But if I keep wearing the new shoes, usually I will break them in and get used to them. Finally the new shoes will feel as comfortable as my old shoes used to feel.

The same is true when I first try to read faster. The new, faster speed feels uncomfortable at first. I just don't feel at ease with this faster speed right away. For a while it might be necessary to force myself to read faster. But if I keep using this faster speed, I will gradually get used to it. Finally the faster speed will feel as comfortable as my old, slower speed used to feel.

Then I can try to boost my speed a little bit more.

I should also keep this in mind: I should not try to boost my speed too much at a time. Each time that I start to raise my speed, I should try to read just a little bit faster than I was reading before. In other words, my speed improvement should be done a small step at a time.

Being able to read faster will help me in many ways. One important way is this: I will be able to study my lessons well much faster than I could before I increased my speed. So now I will have more time left to enjoy hobbies and other kinds of recreation.

Here are things I can do to improve my reading speeds:

2. Do I look at and read just one little word at a time?
I should try to see and read more than one little word at a time.

3. Do I spend too much time looking at each word or group of words?
I should not spend any longer than necessary looking at a word or at a group of words.

4. At times it might be necessary for me to look back over the last few words that I have just read before I continue on to the end of the sentence. Most of the time, however, it is not really necessary for me to look back. Most of the time, my looking back is just a habit. It is a bad habit that makes me read slower than I am really able to read. So I should break that habit, because it hurts me.

5. Do I move my lips or tongue or throat muscles while I read? Do I use any part of my mouth to form the words while I read? If I do any of those things, I should force myself gradually to stop that habit. It might take some time and constant practice, but I must break those habits before I can really speed up my reading. And I can break those habits if I really want to and if I keep trying.
This will help me to break a tongue-moving habit: I can have my tongue place itself between my teeth. Then I should close my teeth until they grip my tongue gently but firmly. This will keep my tongue from moving, but it will not hurt my tongue. I should do this every time I read silently until I have broken the tongue-moving habit completely.
This will help me to break the lip-moving habit: I

can partly and loosely close my fist. Then I can rest my lips gently but firmly against the side of my index finger, with my thumb extended to my cheek. This is a fairly comfortable position, and nobody will suspect that I am trying to break a lip-moving habit. Why? Because a lot of people just naturally read with their hand in a position like that. I should use this trick every time I read silently until I have broken the lip-moving habit completely.

6. Do I point to the words while I read? Do I move my head as though I were watching a tennis match? If I do either of those things, I need to break that habit, too.

7. Suppose I have one of the bad habits that we have been talking about. Suppose that I try to speed up my reading while I still have that bad habit. That would be like a car driver trying to make the car go faster by "stepping on the gas" and pushing down on the brake at the same time. It wouldn't work.

Those bad habits are just like brakes. As long as I have them, they will hold down my reading speed no matter how hard I try to speed up my reading. So I should practice regularly and try to break those habits as soon as possible.

8. These are the only parts of me that I really need in order to read silently: my eyes, my brain, and the nerves that connect them. I can read as fast as I can see and think about what I see. I can see and think a lot faster than those other parts of my body can move.

9. I should not read orally any more than I have to until I have built up my reading speed. If I do a lot of oral reading, that will slow down my reading speed.

10. Improving my reading vocabulary and my reading comprehension will help my reading speed to get better.

11. I should read silently plenty of easy stories, articles, and books. I should make myself read them as fast as I can understand what I am reading.

12. Doing speed lessons and doing timed reading regularly should help me to increase my reading speed.

13. Using a tachistascope correctly and regularly can be helpful. The tachistascope will help me to quicken my ability to understand what I see. It will quicken my thinking. It also will quicken my ability to take action (mental or physical or both) as a result of what I see. All this should help me to increase my reading speed.

14. Using gadgets such as reading accelerators, mechanical devices (machines) for reading and those for skimming, and reading films are helpful to many people. The gadgets must be used correctly and regularly.

15. The most important thing to remember about reading speed is this: I should read as fast as I can understand, but not faster than I can understand.

SECTION 11

SKIMMING — WHAT IS IT?

What is skimming? Skimming is making my eyes go fast across and down a page. While I do this, I am not actually reading. I am looking for something to read.

I can use skimming when I am looking for a fact, a detail, or a bit of information. This kind of skimming sometimes is called scanning.

I can use skimming to get a rough idea what a story, an article, or a book is about.

I am using a kind of skimming when I glance over the pages of a newspaper. I don't have time to read everything in a newspaper, so I glance quickly over the headlines and the illustrations. If my eyes catch a headline that interests me, I'll glance (skim) over the article. If it looks interesting, I'll read that article. If it doesn't look interesting, I'll skip that article and continue to skim.

I use the same sort of skimming to help me find interesting articles and stories in magazines. Here, the table of contents also is a timesaving help.

I also use this kind of skimming when I glance over the table of contents and the other pages of a book. This helps me to decide fairly quickly whether or not I think the book will interest me.

So what is skimming? It is glancing over the pages of things like books and magazines. It is a timesaving skill. If used wisely, skimming is a valuable tool. Why? Because it will help me to do my school work faster, better, and more easily. It also will help me to get more satisfaction from newspapers, magazines, and pleasure books.

The next section (Section 12, "Skimming in Action") explains how to use skimming wisely in three important kinds of school work.

Before we start with a discussion about how to use skimming, though, I'd better be sure that my mind realizes these important facts: Skimming is a skill. Like any other skill that is being developed, it must be used over and over again. So if I practice skimming a lot and practice it right, I will get to be a good skimmer. Then I will know what a valuable

tool skimming is. For day after day I will see how skimming really helps me to do a better job when I am studying,
how it is making my studying easier, and how it is saving
me a lot of time, too.

SECTION 12
SKIMMING IN ACTION

Skim-Preview a Lesson before Reading It

Skimming Helps Me Find Answers for Assigned Questions

Skimming Helps Me Find Information for a Report or for a
Term Paper

Finding Information in Books

Finding Information in Magazines

SKIM-PREVIEW A LESSON BEFORE READING IT

I should skim over a lesson before I start to read the lesson. The skimming gives me a preview of the lesson as a whole. The skimming gives my mind an idea of what it will have to be working on. The skimming also gets my mind warmed up for the lesson.

As I skim along — as my eyes speed across and down the page — things will catch my eye. When this happens, I should slow down and read that, thinking about it and about how it fits into the overall plan of the lesson. Then I start skimming again until something else catches my eyes.

Let's see how that works:

Here is my lesson. I start to skim. The first thing that catches my eyes will be the main title. I read this and think about it. I realize that this is the big main idea that the lesson will discuss or develop. And I wonder just how the author will go about discussing or developing that big main idea. What will be the author's plan of development?

I skim along across and down the page. My eyes are zipping and looking. I'm not actually reading anything right now. Then suddenly something attracts my eyes. It is a subtitle. I slow down and read the subtitle. I think about it and what it means. I realize that the subtitle tells me or suggests to me what the main idea of this section of the lesson is. I notice how this idea is related to the title or main idea of the lesson. I do this for each subtitle. Taken together, the subtitles give me the plan that the author used to develop and discuss the main idea of the whole lesson.

So before I read one word of the lesson itself, I have in my mind the main parts of an outline of the lesson. When I finish skimming over the lesson, my mind has a pretty good idea of what the lesson is mostly about.

While I am skimming over the lesson, other things will catch my eyes, too. Maps, pictures, graphs, diagrams, charts, tables — things like these will catch my eyes. Each time this happens, I should pause briefly to notice what it is about and how it fits into that section of the lesson. Also, I should think of how that illustration will be used to help me understand that section of the lesson better.

When I finish skimming, I will return to the beginning of the lesson and get ready to start reading it.

All of this sounds like a lot of time is being used. Actually, this skimming takes very little time. And in the long run, the skimming saves me time. That is true, because this preview-skimming makes it easier for me to read the lesson. I will be able to understand the lesson, get the main ideas, and get the important bits of information much better if I skim-preview the lesson first. And I will need less time to do the job well.

(Also see "How Should I Study a Lesson?": "Skim-Preview" on pages 24-25, 28-29.)

SKIMMING HELPS ME FIND ANSWERS
FOR ASSIGNED QUESTIONS

Sometimes a teacher assigns a lesson to be studied, and he lists some questions that will be answered in the lesson. I am supposed to study and learn the whole lesson, not just the answers to the questions. Those questions are meant just to guide my thinking while I am reading the lesson. That is the kind of situation we were discussing in "Skim-Preview a Lesson Before Reading It" on pages 78-79, and in Section 6, "How Should I Study a Lesson?" It is **not** the kind of situation that we are getting ready to talk about now.

Here is the situation that we are going to discuss now: The teacher tells the class to answer some questions. He tells the class that the answers are in a certain chapter of the book. I am not supposed to study that chapter. I am not supposed to learn all of the main ideas and important bits of information in the chapter. All that I have to do is to find the answers to those questions — no more than that; no less than that.

Many people start reading at the beginning of the assignment, and they read until they find the answers for the questions. That is **not** the way I should do the kind of assignment that we are talking about. Why? Because it would take me so much more time than I really need to spend on this kind of an assignment.

This is the way I should tackle an assignment like that:

1. I will write the question.

2. I will underline the most important word or words in the question, and I will think about what that word means or what those words mean. The underlined word or words will serve as a clue to help me find where the question is answered. Here are two examples:
    a. What are the main exports of Costa Rica?
    b. Why does San Jose', Costa Rica, have a good climate?
Sometimes the question might not have a really good clue word. Or the question might need another clue word

that is not in the question. When that is true, I must think of a good clue word to use. For example, "How do people get from place to place in <u>Alaska</u>?" In addition to <u>Alaska</u>, I probably will need the word <u>transportation</u> as a clue word.

3. Next, I will start at the beginning of the chapter, and I will skim the chapter. This will make it possible for me to find quickly the place or places where the question is answered. While I skim, I must think about the clue word or words.

As I skim, I will notice and read subtitles. I also will notice illustrations like maps, diagrams, graphs, pictures, charts, and tables, and I will read their captions.

In just a few seconds, I usually can find the section or the illustrations where my question will be answered. The subtitles and the captions will tell me.

I will skim the whole chapter, because my question might be answered partly in one place and partly in another place.

4. What should I do when I find the section where my question will be answered?

First, I will think about the question. I will think especially about the clue word or words and about what kind of question I have to answer. When I say "<u>what kind of question</u> I have to answer," I mean this: If <u>the question asks,</u> "<u>When</u> did. . .?" I will look for a <u>time</u> answer, such as a date; if the question asks, "<u>Who</u> did. . .?" I will look for a name; etc.

Now I will skim down the section until my eyes see information that might answer the question. I will stop skimming, and I will read the sentence quickly. If that information does not answer or help answer the question, I'll continue skimming until my eyes again see information that might answer the question. I'll continue to do this until I find where the answer to the question is located.

5. Then I'll read the sentence or sentences that answer the question. (I might find it necessary to go up a paragraph or two in order to get to the place where the information begins. And I should be sure to continue reading as long as there is a possibility that a paragraph has information that I need). I will read fairly fast — just to get a general idea of

what the information is like.

6. Then I will reread the sentence or sentences that have the information I need. This time I will read more slowly and carefully. I will take notes or I will write the information in my own words. If necessary, I will write the information as a direct quotation, being careful to use quotation marks.

7. My answer should have all of the information that is necessary to answer the question. At the same time, my answer should leave out information that does not help to answer the question. If I am not sure whether or not to use a certain bit of information, I will do this: I will turn the question into the first part of the answer. (For example: Why does San Jose', Costa Rica, have a good climate? ➡ San Jose', Costa Rica, has a good climate because. . . .) Now, if the information will complete the sentence correctly and sensibly, I will use that information. If the information will not complete the sentence correctly and sensibly, I will not use that information.

8. When I get all of the questions answered, I will rewrite the questions and the answers so that my paper will be neat, and my answers will be accurate and complete.

Now here is an easy-to-use, step-by-step summary of what I should do to find answers for assigned questions:

1. I will write the question.

2. I will underline the clue word or words in the question, and I will think about what that word means or what those words mean. I also might have to think of a clue word that is not actually in the question:
    a. What are the main exports of Costa Rica?
    b. Why does San Jose', Costa Rica, have a good climate?
    c. How do people get from place to place in Alaska? (also transportation)

3. I will skim the pages to find quickly the subtitle of the paragraphs where the answer will be located. While I

skim, I must think about the clue word or words.

I must remember that the answer might be located under more than one subtitle.

I must remember, also, that the answer might be found in an illustration like a map, diagram, chart, graph, table, or picture. So I must be sure to notice them and to read the captions under them.

4. I will think about the question. I will think especially about the clue word or words and about what kind of question I have to get answered. Then I will skim down the paragraphs until I spot the place where the question is answered.

5. I will read the sentence or sentences that answer the question. I will read fairly fast. I will read just to get a general idea of what the information is like. (I will be sure to start reading where the information begins, and I will be sure to continue reading until I reach the end of the information.)

6. I will reread the sentence or sentences. This time I will read more slowly and carefully. I will take notes or I will write in my own words the information that I need. If it is necessary to use the exact words of the book, I must use quotation marks at the beginning and at the end of the words.

7. If I am not sure whether or not to use a certain bit of information, I will do this: I will turn the question into the first part of the answer. If the information will complete the sentence correctly and sensibly, I will use that information. If the information will not complete the sentence correctly and sensibly, I will not use that information:

    a. The main exports of Costa Rica are. . . .

    b. San Jose', Costa Rica, has a good climate because. . . .

    c. People get from place to place in Alaska by. . . .

8. Finally, I will rewrite the questions and the answers so that they are complete, accurate, and neat.

Sometimes a teacher might assign questions to be answered. The answers are somewhere in the textbook, but the teacher did not say where — he did not say what chapter or chapters to use. What should I do?

This is what I should do:

I will use steps 1 and 2 in the outline that we have been talking about.

Then I will use the index and, if necessary, the table of contents in order to find out the approximate location of the answers.

Then I will use the rest of the steps in the outline, starting now with step 3.

It also is possible for the teacher to assign questions to be answered, but the answers are not in the textbook. In a situation like that, I should use the advice given next in "Skimming Helps Me Find Information for a Report or for a Term Paper".

SKIMMING HELPS ME FIND INFORMATION FOR A REPORT OR FOR A TERM PAPER

The problem here is this: I have to write a report or a term paper. I know the topic that I have to write about. But I have no idea where to find the information that I need.

There are several ways that I can go about getting the information that I need:

I can make an appointment with somebody who is an expert on that subject. In this way, I can interview the person and thus get first-hand information.

I can write to an expert and ask for information.

Depending on the kind of report that I have to make, there are other places where I can get information in person or by letter — places like a chamber of commerce (city, state, or United States); a museum; a city, county, state, or federal government office, including the United States Government Printing Office (see the next paragraph); a business or a labor organization; a representative of a foreign country.

The United States Government Printing Office has free price lists that describe each book or pamphlet that it can send. When I write for a price list, I should write to the Superintendent of Documents, U. S. Government Printing Office, Washington, D. C. 20402. On my request, I should write the number and title of each price list that I need. Here are the price lists that were available when Johnny's Reading Skills went to press:

Number	Title	Number	Title
10	Laws, Rules and Regulations	33 A	Occupations
11	Home Economics	35	National Parks
15	Geology	36	Government Periodicals and Subscription Services
19	Army		
21	Fish and Wildlife	37	Tariff and Taxation
25	Transportation, Highways, and Roads	38	Animal Industry
		41	Insects
28	Finance	42	Irrigation, Draining, Water Power
31	Education		
33	Labor	43	Forestry

Number	Title	Number	Title
44	Plants	64	Scientific Tests, Standards
46	Soils and Fertilizers	65	Foreign Relations of U. S.
48	Weather, Astronomy, and Meteorology	67	Immigration, Naturalization, and Citizenship
50	American History	68	Farm Management
51	Health and Hygiene	70	Census
51 A	Diseases	71	Children's Bureau
53	Maps	72	Homes
54	Political Science	78	Industrial Workers
55	Indians	79	Aviation
58	Mines	81	Posters and Charts
59	Interstate Commerce	82	Radio and Electricity
60	Guam, Puerto Rico, Samoa, and Virgin Islands	83	Library of Congress
62	Commerce	84	Atomic Energy and Civil Defense
63	Navy, Marine Corps, and Coast Guard	85	Defense, Veterans' Affairs

I can get information by experimenting and by observation.

I can get information from lectures.

I can get information from exhibits and from such things as maps, models, pictures, and posters.

I can get information from movies, from radio, and from television.

I can get information from an encyclopedia.

I can get information from almanacs and from yearbooks.

I can get information from newspapers, magazines, pamphlets, and books.

The rest of this discussion will concentrate on how to get information from books. Later, we will mention using magazines as a possible source of information.

Finding Information in Books

1. First I will go to the library.

2. Using the card catalog, I will make a list of the

books that might have information about my topic. I will write the call number, author's name, title, and copyright date for each book as I list it. This information (except for the date) will help me to find the books quickly. The date is important, because usually I will want the most up-t -date information that I can find.

3. Now I will get the books that are on my list and take them to a table.

4. I will select one of the books, and I will turn to its index. I will keep in mind the different possible ways that my topic might be listed in the index. Then I will skim down the index to see whether or not this book appears to have information that I can use in my report.

5. If the index does not seem to have my topic listed in any way, I will check the table of contents. The table of contents will indicate whether or not the book discusses a subject that might include the topic that I am working on.

6. Suppose I can find no indication either in the index or in the table of contents that the book has information that I need. Then I will put this book aside and try the next book.

7. However, suppose that either the index or the table of contents indicates that the book does discuss my topic or a subject that might include my topic. Then I will turn to the page where the discussion begins.

8. Now, keeping in my mind what I am looking for, I will skim down the page (and, if necessary, the pages) until I find the place where the information that I need begins.

9. Then I will read the paragraph or paragraphs that have the information that I need. I will read fairly fast. I am reading now just to get a general idea of what the information is like.

10. I will turn back to the place where my information begins. I will reread the paragraph or paragraphs. This time I will read more slowly and carefully. I will take notes or I will write the information in my own words. If any of

the information should be used exactly as it is written in the book, I will write it down as a direct quotation, being careful to use quotation marks. I also will write down the page number or numbers, so I will know exactly where I found the information in that book.

I will use steps 1, 2, and 3. Then I will use steps 4 - 6 or steps 4 - 10 for each book on my list until I have all of the information that I need.

Now here is an easy-to-use, step-by-step summary of what I should do to find information in a book for a report or for a term paper:

1. I will go to the library.

2. Using the card catalog, I will make a list of the books that might have information about my topic. I will write the call number, author's name, title, and copyright date for each book as I list it.

3. I will get the books that are on my list.

4. I will check the index (skimming and thinking) to see if the book appears to have any information about my topic.

5. I will check the table of contents if the index does not seem to have my topic listed in any way.

6. If my topic apparently is not discussed in that book, I will put the book to one side.

7. If the index or the table of contents indicates that the book discusses my topic, I will turn to the page where the discussion begins.

8. I will keep in mind what I am looking for, and I will skim down the page (or pages) until I find the place where the information begins.

9. I will read the paragraph or paragraphs that have the information I need. I will read fairly fast. I will read

just to get a general idea of what the information is like.

10. I will reread the paragraph or paragraphs. I will read more slowly and more carefully. I will take notes, or I will write the information in my own words. I will use the exact words of the book only when necessary, being careful to use quotation marks. I also will write down the page number or numbers to show exactly where I got the information in that book.

Finding Information in Magazines

The steps are very similar to the steps that I use to find information in books.

Here are the steps:

1. I will go to the library.

2. Using the Readers' Guide to Periodical Literature, I will list each magazine article that might discuss my topic. I will write the author's name, title of the article, name of the magazine, volume number of the magazine (and the issue number, if there is an issue number), number of the page where the article begins, and the date of the magazine.

3. I will get the magazine or the magazines that are on my list.

4. I will turn to the beginning of the first article on my list.

5.
6.   I will use steps 8, 9, and 10 for "Finding Information in Books".
7.

PART II

WORD STUDY

SECTION 13

ALPHABET	CONSONANTS	VOWELS
a		a
b	b	
c	c	
d	d	
e		e
f	f	
g	g	
h	h	
i		i
j	j	
k	k	
l	l	
m	m	
n	n	
o		o
p	p	
q	q	
r	r	
s	s	
t	t	
u		u
v	v	
w	w	
x	x	
y	y (sometimes)	y (sometimes)
z	z	

SECTION 14
CONSONANTS

Consonants and Their Sounds

Consonants That Like To Be Different

Some Consonants Blend

Some Consonants Make Teams

Some Consonants Are Silent Sometimes

CONSONANTS AND THEIR SOUNDS

Each consonant has the sound that I hear at the beginning of its sample word:

b	boy
c	(See "Consonants That Like To Be Different.")
d	(See "Consonants That Like To Be Different.")
f	fish
g	(See "Consonants That Like To Be Different.")
h	him
j	jam
k	kind
l	like
m	more
n	now
p	pay
q	(See "Consonants That Like To Be Different.")
r	read
s	(See "Consonants That Like To Be Different.")
t	(See "Consonants That Like To Be Different.")
v	vote
w	we
x	(See "Consonants That Like To Be Different.")
y	(See "Consonants That Like To Be Different.")
z	zoo

CONSONANTS THAT LIKE TO BE DIFFERENT

Most of the consonants use only one sound. For example, b has the sound that I hear at the beginning of the word boy. B has this same sound if it comes at the beginning of a word, in the middle of a word (rab-bit), or at the end of a word (tub). This is true of most consonants. So once I learn the sound of one of those consonants, that is the sound I will use for that consonant.

But a few consonants like to be different. Some of them are not satisfied with one sound, and two of them (q and x) use a double sound. These are the consonants that we are going to investigate now.

1. Sounds of c
    c is using the k sound: cake, club, pic-nic
    c is using the s sound: cent, city, cyclone, nice

    c has no sound of its own. It always must borrow a sound. Sometimes c borrows from k, and sometimes c borrows from s.
    Usually, I will make c sound hard (like k) if e or i or y does not come right after the c.
    Usually, I will make c sound soft (like s) if e or i or y does come right after the c.

    Reminder to teachers: Remember that c also might use the sh sound, when c is followed by i. This happens in these vowel-consonant teams, which often are found in the last syllable of a word or of a root word: cial, cian, cient, and cious.
    Once in a while, c followed by i might use the sh sound when it is not a part of one of those teams: ap-pre-ci-ate. Also, c followed by e might use the sh sound: o-cean. But these are isolated cases. Such cases seldom happen. The latter is very rare. Neither case happens at all at the beginning of a word.
    Even more rare is the situation in which c followed by e uses the ch sound: cello.

2. Sounds of d: d̲ is using the d̲ sound: d̲ime, d̲id̲, d̲og

Almost all of the time I will make d̲ use its own sound.

Reminder to teachers: Remember that d also might use the j̲ sound when d is followed by u̲: ed-u̲-c̄ate, sched-ule. The d̄ + u situation does not occur in many words, but when it does occur, d̲ is likely to use the j̲ sound. That is not true at the beginning of a word, however. If a word starts with d̲u, d will use its own sound.
Remember, also, that the d of an e̲d̲ ending might sound like t̲ sometimes to some people. See pages 167-168.

3. Sounds of g

g is using the g̲ sound (as in g̲o): g̲ate, g̲lad, bug̲

g̲ is using the j̲ sound: g̲erm, g̲iant, g̲ypsy, ag̲e

Sometimes g̲ uses its own sound. But sometimes g̲ borrows the sound of j.
Usually, I will make g̲ sound hard (this is g's own sound, like g̲ in g̲o) if e̲ or i̲ or y̲ does not come right after the g̲.
Usually, I will make g̲ sound soft (like j̲) if e̲ or i̲ or y̲ does come right after the g̲.

4. Sound of q: q̲ has no sound of its own.
u̲ always comes right after q̲.
The q̲u̲ sounds like k̲w̲: q̲uick, q̲uack.

5. Sounds of s

s̲ is using the s̲ sound: s̲aw, us̲, in-s̲ect

s̲ is using the z̲ sound: is̲, nos̲e, rai-s̲in

I should make s̲ use the s̲ sound at the beginning of a word.
I might make s̲ use the s̲ sound or the z̲ sound when s̲ is in the middle of a word or at the end of a word.

Reminder to teachers: Remember that s̲ also might

use the sh sound when s is followed by i. This happens in one of the sion vowel-consonant teams, often found in the last syllable of a word or of a root word: com-pre-hen-sion. In the other sion teams, s has a sound that is neither the s sound nor the sh sound: con-clu-sion.

Once in a while, s followed by u might sound like sh: sure. But this is an isolated case — it rarely happens.

Even more rare is the situation in which s followed by u sounds like the s in the second sion team mentioned above: u-su-al.

6. Sounds of t: t is using the t sound: time, hat, un-til

Most of the time I will make t use the t sound.

Reminder to teachers: Remember that t followed by i might use the sh sound. This happens in these vowel-consonant teams, which are found often in the last syllable of a word or of a root word: tial, tient, tion, and tious.

Once in a while, t followed by i might use the sh sound when it is not a part of one of those teams: ne-go-ti-ate. But this is an isolated case — it rarely happens. It does not happen at all at the beginning of a word.

Remember, also, that t followed by u might use the ch sound. This happens when ture is a vowel-consonant team. The ture is found often at the end of a word or of a root word.

In addition, t followed by u might use the ch sound when it is not a part of the ture team: for-tune. This does not happen at the beginning of a word, and it does not happen in the stu combination at the beginning of a word.

7. Sound of x: x has no sound of its own.
                 x sounds like ks: ax, box, fix

8. Sounds of y: y is not satisfied being just a consonant.
                  y likes to be a vowel, too.

This is information about consonant y:

y is at the beginning of a word. I will make y use its consonant sound: yard, yes, yet.

y is at the beginning of a syllable inside a word. I

usually will make y̲ use its consonant sound: be-yo̲nd, can-yo̲n, law-yer̲.

Information about vowel y̲ is on page 110, in the vowel section of this book.

SOME CONSONANTS BLEND

We have a consonant blend when two or three consonants are right together, and each of those consonants uses its own sound. When I pronounce the word, I can hear the sound of each consonant that is in the blend.

If I know what each consonant in the alphabet sounds like, then it will be easy for me to sound out the consonant blend part of a word that I don't recognize. Because all I do is say the sound of the first consonant, then the sound of the next consonant, then the sound of the vowel, etc. Each sound hooks itself onto the next sound with no stops or pauses until I have sounded the whole syllable or all of the one-syllable word. I must just be sure not to stop or pause or say a sound like "uh" between the sounds of the letters.

Here are double consonant blends:

1. black	13. scout
2. brick	14. skin
3. clean	15. sleep
4. crate	16. smile
5. dress	17. snake
6. dwell	18. spell
7. flag	19. squeal
8. free	20. stand
9. glad	21. swing
10. grade	22. tree
11. play	23. twenty
12. prize	

Here are triple consonant blends:

1. scream	3. spring
2. splash	4. street

Here are some consonant blends at the end of words:

1.	draft	10.	scarf
2.	hold	11.	bark
3.	self	12.	farm
4.	help	13.	barn
5.	felt	14.	sharp
6.	camp	15.	part
7.	band	16.	task
8.	print	17.	gasp
9.	cord	18.	best

Here are some consonant blends in the middle of words:

1.	em-blem	8.	ex-plain
2.	in-clude	9.	sur-prise
3.	in-crease	10.	sub-scribe
4.	ad-dress	11.	re-spect
5.	in-flate	12.	ham-ster
6.	a-glow	13.	in-struct
7.	a-gree	14.	at-tract

SOME CONSONANTS MAKE TEAMS

We have a consonant team when two consonants are right together, and together they are silent, or together they make a sound that we would not expect them to make — a sound that usually is different from either of the two consonants.

These consonant teams are in many words. So it is necessary for me to learn each team and to remember what each team might do in a word.

If I don't know these teams, I will have trouble recognizing many words. I also will have trouble trying to figure out words that I don't recognize.

If I do know these teams, it will be a lot easier for me to recognize words. It also will be a lot easier for me to figure out words that I don't recognize.

Here are the consonant teams:

1. ch
   ch is using the ch sound: chair, chin, arch
   ch is using the k sound: chorus, ache, stomach

Usually, I will make ch use the ch sound. But if this does not work, I will make ch use the k sound.

Reminder to teachers: Remember that sometimes ch might use the sh sound. Words in which this happens usually are words that have come to us from the French language: chef.

2. gh
   gh is using no sound; gh is silent: high, caught, bought
   gh is using the f sound: enough, laugh, rough

I should try first to make gh keep silent (especially if t comes right after gh). But if this doesn't work, I will make gh use the f sound.

Once in a while, gh might sound like hard g — the g sound in go: ghost, a-ghast. This does not happen often.

3. ph: Sounds like <u>f</u>: <u>ph</u>one, gra<u>ph</u>, go-<u>ph</u>er

4. sh: If I have just gotten the baby to go to sleep, it's the sound that I might make to tell somebody to be quiet: <u>sh</u>e, <u>sh</u>ade, fi<u>sh</u>.

one <u>th</u> sound: <u>th</u>is, smoo<u>th</u>, ei-<u>th</u>er

5. th

the other <u>th</u> sound: <u>th</u>in, wi<u>th</u>, a<u>th</u>-lete

When I say the first <u>th</u> sound, I hear a vibrating sound, but I don't hear or feel much air leaving my mouth.

When I say the second <u>th</u> sound, I don't hear a vibrating sound, but I hear and feel a lot of air rushing from my mouth.

I am sounding out a word that I don't recognize. I see <u>th</u> in the word. If the first <u>th</u> sound doesn't work, I should try the other <u>th</u> sound.

6. wh: It's a very quiet sound. Actually, it's not much of a sound at all. If I touch something hot, pull back my finger and blow on it to cool the burned spot, I am making the <u>wh</u> sound: <u>wh</u>en, <u>wh</u>ile, <u>wh</u>ite.

Those consonant teams all end with <u>h</u>. There are two other consonant teams, but they don't end with <u>h</u>. Here they are:

7. ng: I hear the <u>ng</u> sound in these words: lo<u>ng</u>, ra<u>ng</u>, si<u>ng</u>.

8. nk: I hear the <u>nk</u> sound in these words: ba<u>nk</u>, i<u>nk</u>, su<u>nk</u>. I can hear <u>k</u> making the <u>k</u> sound, so it seems as though <u>nk</u> wouldn't <u>be</u> a team. But notice that when <u>n</u> and k are together, the <u>n</u> doesn't sound like <u>n</u>. So when <u>n</u> and <u>k</u> are together, they <u>do</u> form a team.

SOME CONSONANTS ARE SILENT SOMETIMES

Some consonants that come together in a syllable or in a one-syllable word will not blend their sounds, so they will not form a consonant blend. They do not team together as the consonants in a consonant team do, so they will not form a consonant team. Actually, they will not work together at all, so one of them usually keeps silent.

Here are some of them:

1. bt   at the end of a word:
         b is silent: debt, doubt

2. gn   at the beginning of a word or at the end of a word:
         g is silent: gnat, sign
            In the middle of a word, gn might sound like ny: mi-gnon (min-yon), or g and n might be di-vided, with each using its own sound: di-ag-nose.

3. kn   at the beginning of a word:
         k is silent: knee, knife

4. lk   in some words:
         l is silent: talk, folks
            But in some words l is not silent: elk, milk.

5. mb   at the end of a word:
         b is silent: climb, thumb

6. mn   at the end of a word:
         n is silent: column, hymn

7. pn   at the beginning of a word:
         p is silent: pneu-mat-ic, pneu-mo-nia

8. ps   at the beginning of a word:
         p is silent: psalm, psy-chol-o-gy

9. pt   at the beginning of a word:
         p is silent: pto-maine, pty-a-lin

10. rh   h is silent: rhyme, rhu-barb

But not in compound words when the first word ends with r and the second word starts with h: carhop; and not if a prefix ends with r and the root word begins with h: superhuman.

11. st   in the middle of some words:

t might be silent (examples are at the end of the last paragraph)

At the beginning of a word, st forms a consonant blend: stamp.

At the end of a word, st forms a consonant blend: best.

In the middle of a word, st is tricky. If st is with another consonant in the middle of a word, usually st will stay together in a syllable and make a consonant blend: lob-ster. If s and t are the only consonants together in the middle of a word, they might go into different syllables, and both might have a sound: pas-tel; or t might be silent: cas-tle, lis-ten.

12. wr   w is silent: wrap, write

Inside some words, this might happen: w might help form a vowel-consonant team with the vowel before w: dow-ry.

13. Double consonants at the end of a word:

The last consonant is silent: miss, tell.

14. Double consonants in the middle of a word: fun-ny, sup-per

Many dictionaries and texts indicate or say that one of the consonants (usually the second consonant) is silent. However, we have found in actual practice that the majority of our pupils hear both consonants, or at least they think that they hear both consonants. For this reason, we no longer include this situation in our study.

Some more examples of silent consonants are given in Section 16, "Freaks", on pages 135-137.

SECTION 15

VOWELS

Introduction to Vowels

When Y Is a Vowel
  When Is Y a Vowel?
  What Vowel Y Does

Long Vowel Sounds
  When Should I Use a Long Vowel Sound?

Short Vowel Sounds
  When Should I Use a Short Vowel Sound?

Regular Exceptions to the Vowel Sound Clues

Vowel Sound Teams and Vowel-Consonant Teams
  Major Teams
  Minor Teams

Vowels in Unaccented Syllables

Summary of Vowel Sounds

INTRODUCTION TO VOWELS

It is not easy to learn about the sounds of vowels in our language, but I can learn about them if I really try. And I must learn about them if I am going to be able to figure out words that I don't recognize.

In order to learn about the sounds of the vowels in our language, I will need information, and I will need plenty of practice using that information.

Using information regularly and often helps me to understand what the information is all about. That is why practice is so necessary. That is why I should practice using the vowel sound information every chance I get. The more I use it, the better I will understand it. Together, the information about vowel sounds and the practice using that information will help me to understand better how vowels work in our language. That understanding is very important.

This section of Johnny's Reading Skills will give me the information that I need about vowels and vowel sounds. Whether or not I bring this information into my brain and learn it depends mostly on me. Whether or not I use that information and put it to work for me in actual day after day practice depends mostly on me. So whether or not I get the necessary understanding also depends mostly on me. When I do get that understanding, I will be able to work with vowels more easily, and I will have more confidence in myself.

This is why it is not easy to learn about vowels and their sounds: There are so many exceptions to the clues (rules) that are supposed to tell us what sounds to make when we are figuring out a word. This is a real problem.

So long as our language stays the way it is, we know of no way to solve this problem completely. But we can make the problem a lot easier to handle. Then it will be easier to get the information that we need about vowels and their sounds. It then will be easier to practice using that information. Finally, it will be easier to understand how vowels work.

We said that we have a problem with vowels and their sounds because there are so many exceptions to the clues (rules). The clues tell us when we should use a long vowel sound and when we should use a short vowel sound. Some-times, though, the clue says, "Use a long vowel sound". But we can't. Instead, we have to use a short vowel sound. Another time the clue might say, "Use a short vowel sound". Instead, we find that we have to use a long vowel sound. At other times, we can use neither a long vowel sound nor a short vowel sound. Instead, we have to use some special sound for the vowel.

Here is what we will do to attack the vowel sound prob-lem and make it easier to handle: First, we will learn thor-oughly the long vowel sounds and the long vowel sound clues. Next, we will learn thoroughly the short vowel sounds and the short vowel sound clue. Now, since the whole problem is caused by exceptions, we will try to organize those ex-ceptions in a way that will be as simple and as logical as possible. Once we do that, then our vowel sound problem will be organized. It will not be so all scattered around. Then the information about vowels and their sounds will be a lot easier to learn, use, and understand.

Here, then, is how we will organize our vowel sound study:

First, there are the Long Vowel Sounds and the Long Vowel Sound Clues.

Then there are the Short Vowel Sounds and the Short Vowel Sound Clue.

There are what we will call the Regular Exceptions to the Vowel Sound Clues.

We have what we will call Vowel Sound Teams and Vowel-Consonant Teams.

There are the sounds that the vowels often make in syl-lables that are not accented. These are our Vowels in Un-accented Syllables.

Finally, there are words that cannot be put into any of the groups that we have listed. We will call these words Freaks, and we will talk about them in Section 16.

We will examine and discuss each of those vowel sound groups in this section of the book. Before we do, however, we will investigate <u>vowel y</u>.

WHEN Y IS A VOWEL

Pages 98-99 told me about y when y is a consonant.

Now I have two questions about y as a vowel: When is y a vowel? What do I do with y when y is a vowel?

When Is Y a Vowel?

Y is inside a word; it is not at the beginning of a sylla-ble in the word. Usually, I will make y act like a vowel.

Y is at the end of a word. I will make y act like a vowel.

What Vowel Y Does

Y is at the end of a word that has two or more syllables; the last syllable is not accented. Y will sound like short i to some ears, but y will sound like long e to other ears. (Which of the two a person hears seems to depend on how the person's talking and hearing have been trained): can'-dy, don'-key, po'-ny, a-bil'-i-ty.

At all other times when y is a vowel, I will treat y the same as i. That is true, because vowel y is like a substitute i: my, re-ply', cy'-clone, pay'-ment, rhyme, cyl'-in-der.

LONG VOWEL SOUNDS

Each vowel has two main sounds: 1) long and 2) short.

A vowel is long when it says its name. That is, when I say the name of a vowel, I am saying the long sound of that vowel. So when I need to use the long sound of a vowel, I will use the sound which is the same as the name of that vowel.

These, then, are the long vowel sounds — the long vowel sound is the sound that I hear at the beginning of each of these words:

long a:	ate
long e:	eat
long i:	I'm
long o:	oats
long u:	use

When Should I Use a Long Vowel Sound?

Clue 1.

The Clue: There are two vowels together in the syllable.

What I Do: Usually, I will make the first vowel use its long sound, and I will make the second vowel be silent:

aim	play	meat	rea-son
east	fee	feet	con-tain
oak	hoe	boat	re-peat

Clue 2.

The Clue: There are two vowels in the syllable. The two vowels are not together. The second vowel is e, and the e is at the end of the syllable.

What I Do: Usually, I will make the first vowel use its long sound, and I will make the e on the end be silent:

ate	tape	pine	in-flame
eve	mile	rhyme	con-crete
use	tube	rope	um-pire

Clue 3.

The Clue: There is only one vowel in the syllable. The vowel is at the end of the syllable.

What I Do: Usually, I will make the vowel use its long sound:

me	a-go	se-cret	mo-ment
by	pa-per	fi-nal	hu-man
so	fe-ver	mi-nus	mu-sic

SHORT VOWEL SOUNDS

The short sound of each vowel sounds like this:

Short a:	ant
Short e:	echo
Short i:	it
Short o:	ox
Short u:	us

When Should I Use a Short Vowel Sound?

The Clue: There is only one vowel in the syllable. The vowel is not at the end of the syllable.

What I Do: Usually, I will make the vowel use its short sound:

at	bat	ac-cept
end	bend	rab-bit
in	tin	mis-take
ox	box	con-crete
up	cup	pub-lic

REGULAR EXCEPTIONS
TO THE VOWEL SOUND CLUES

We call these exceptions <u>regular</u> exceptions to the vowel sound clues, because they happen fairly often. That is, they take place with a certain amount of regularity.

Let's see how they work:

Here is a word that I don't recognize. I am trying to figure out what the word is. The vowels do not form a team (vowel teams will be explained in the next section). I try to use one of the long vowel sound clues or the short vowel sound clue, but the clue just doesn't work. What should I do next?

Often, in a case like that, the vowel sound will be the opposite of what the clue says it should be. So, often I will do the opposite of what the clue says I should do.

Notice what happens in these regular exceptions:

1. a. The clue says that the first vowel should be long and the second vowel should be silent. But the opposite of that is happening: The first vowel is silent, and the second vowel is long:

neu-tral   chief   field   be-lief

Should be: long,   silent
Is: silent, long

b. The clue says that the first vowel should be long and the second vowel should be silent. But the first vowel does not have its long sound. Instead, the first vowel is using its short sound, and the second vowel is silent:

death   thread   in-stead   mis-chief

Should be: long,   silent
Is: short, silent

c. The clue says that the first vowel should be long and the second vowel should be silent. But this time the two

vowels are going to do the opposite of what they did in paragraph b above: This time the first vowel will be silent, and
the second vowel will use its short sound:

guess   built   friend   rough

Should be: long,   silent
Is: silent, short

     d. The clue says that the first vowel should be long
and the second vowel should be silent. But this time we split
the vowels apart, and each vowel has a sound:

gi-ant   cre-ate   di-et   qui-et

Should be: long,   silent
Is: a sound ʌ a sound

     Most vowel groups might split apart sometimes.
Some of those vowel groups split apart very seldom, but
others split apart very often. For example, ae almost never
splits apart, but ia splits apart a lot of times. In fact, ia
splits apart more often than any other vowel group. Other
vowels that often split apart are iu and io. Three vowel
groups usually do not split apart, but they do split apart
often enough to make it worthwhile to mention them. They
are ie, ea, and eo.
     These vowel groups are not used as often, but when
they are used they often split apart: ua, ue, ui, uo, and uu.

     2. The clue says that the first vowel should be long and
the e on the end should be silent. But the first vowel is
short, and the e on the end is silent:

since   glance   plunge   con-vince

Should be: long . . . silent e
Is: short. . . silent e

     3. The clue says to make a vowel use its long sound
when it is the only vowel in the syllable and it is at the end
of the syllable. But the vowel is not using its long sound

this time. Instead, the vowel is using its short sound:

ad-di-tion   am-bi-tious   pre-cious   suf-fi-cient

Should be: long
Is: short

4. The clue says to make a vowel use its short sound when it is the only vowel in the syllable and it is not at the end of the syllable. But the vowel is not using its short sound this time. Instead, the vowel is using its long sound:

old   gold   mind   dan-ger

Should be: short
Is: long

VOWEL SOUND TEAMS
AND
VOWEL-CONSONANT TEAMS

Sometimes a vowel sound clue does not work because one of the regular exceptions to the clue is working in that particular case. We have just finished discussing those regular exceptions.

A lot of times, though, the vowel sound clue will not work and neither will the regular exception. The reason often is that a vowel sound team or a vowel-consonant team is working instead of the clue or the regular exception.

What is a vowel sound team? Well, a vowel sound team is made of two vowels that work together as a team. Together they make a vowel sound that is not a long vowel sound and not a short vowel sound. When those two vowels come together in a word, they usually will make that particular sound.

And what is a vowel-consonant team? Well, we have a vowel-consonant team when certain vowels and consonants come together to form a pattern of sounds that we would not ordinarily expect them to make. When those vowels and consonants come together in a word, they usually will make that particular sound pattern.

These teams are in very many words. That is why the teams are so important.

If I know the teams, it will be easier to remember and to recognize words. It also will be easier to figure out words that I don't recognize.

Therefore, I should know these teams so well that I will recognize them and identify them instantly.

Here are the vowel sound teams and the vowel-consonant teams:

Major Teams

The major teams occur in many words or they occur in

words that are used often.

1.   age   will be at the end of the last syllable of a word or of a root word.

The <u>age</u> team sounds like <u>ij</u>:

bag-g<u>age</u>   cot-t<u>age</u>   im-<u>age</u>   scrim-m<u>age</u>

2.   ar   The <u>ar</u> team sounds like the <u>name</u> of this let-ter — R:

<u>ar</u>t   h<u>ar</u>-vest   m<u>ar</u>ch   re-m<u>ar</u>k

SPECIAL CASES OF a r
FOR ADVANCED STUDENTS

The <u>ar</u> is in an accented syllable; another r comes right after the <u>ar</u>, and the r is at the beginning of the next syllable. The <u>ar</u> usually will not use its team sound. Instead, the <u>a</u> usually will use its short a sound: <u>ar</u>'-row, n<u>ar</u>'-ra-tive, em-b<u>ar</u>'-rass.

The <u>ar</u> is in an accented syllable; a vowel comes right after <u>ar</u>, and the vowel is at the beginning of the next syllable. The <u>ar</u> usually will not use its team sound. Instead, <u>a</u> usually will do one of two things:

a. Here is situation <u>a</u>: The <u>ar</u> is inside a word (that is, the <u>ar</u> is not in the first or the last syllable of the word); the <u>ar</u> is in a syllable that has a <u>secondary</u> accent (see page 175); an <u>i</u> or <u>y</u> comes right after <u>ar</u>, and the i or y is at the beginning of the next syllable. In this situation, the <u>a</u> usually will sound like short e.   That will make <u>ar</u> sound like <u>air</u>: dic'-tion-<u>ar</u>'-y, or'-di-n<u>ar</u>'-y, tem'-po-r<u>ar</u>'-i-ly.

b. Here is situation <u>b</u>: Except for the exact situation described in paragraph <u>a</u> above, these facts together make situation b: The <u>ar</u> is in any accented syllable; a vowel (any vowel) comes right after <u>ar</u>, and the vowel is at the beginning of the next syllable. In this situation, the <u>a</u> usually will use its short a sound: p<u>ar</u>'-a-graph; com-p<u>ar</u>'-i-son (Notice this: The <u>ar</u> is inside the word, and <u>i</u> comes right after <u>ar</u>, and the <u>i</u> is at the beginning of the next syllable — just like in situation a. But the ar syllable does NOT have a second-ary accent. Therefore, this is not an example of situation a); par'-en-thet'-ic (Notice this: The ar syllable has a secondary accent. But ar is in the first syllable of the word, and the next syllable does NOT start with i or y. Therefore, this is not an example of situation a); sin'-gu-lar'-i-ty (see the note for the word comparison, starting on page 118).

There is w just before ar in a one-syllable word. The ar usually will not use its team sound. Instead, the ar usually will sound like or: warn, wart, swarm.

In a word with more than one syllable: The w comes just before ar in the same syllable; that syllable is ac-cented. The ar usually will not use its team sound. Instead, ar usually will sound like or: ward'-en, a-ward', a-thwart'.

The ar is in an unaccented syllable. Here are the main situations which might be found:
The ar is in the first syllable of a word; the first syllable is not accented. The ar usually will sound like ar: ar-tis'-tic, car-na'-tion. Once in a while the ar might sound like a short u said very fast and with very little force: ar-rive'. That second situation does not happen often.
The ar is in an unaccented syllable; the ar is not in the first syllable of the word. The ar usually will sound like the er, ir, ur teams said very fast and with very little force: gram'-mar, leth'-ar-gy, par-tic'-u-lar, cir'-cu-lar-ize', for'-ward.

3. are in a word: Sounds like the word air:

dare   rare   share   pre-pare

4. au } They have the sound that I hear in these words:
   aw }

au-to   au-tumn   haul   fault
aw-ful   saw   draw   crawl

5. aw   (See au, aw)

6. cial ⎫
   tial ⎭ will be at the end of the last syllable of a word or of a root word.

They sound a lot like <u>shul</u> said very fast and with very little force:

fa-<u>cial</u>   so-<u>cial</u>   gla-<u>cial</u>   fi-nan-<u>cial</u>

par-<u>tial</u>   es-sen-<u>tial</u>   sub-stan-<u>tial</u>
pres-i-<u>den</u>-<u>tial</u>

7. cian   will be at the end of the last syllable of a word or of a root word.

The <u>cian</u> team sounds a lot like <u>shun</u> said very fast and with very little force:

ma-gi-<u>cian</u>   mu-si-<u>cian</u>   phy-si-<u>cian</u>
e-lec-tri-<u>cian</u>

8. cious ⎫
   tious ⎭ will be at the end of the last syllable of a word or of a root word.

They sound a lot like <u>shus</u> said very fast and with very little force:

con-<u>scious</u> gra-<u>cious</u> pre-<u>cious</u> a-tro-<u>cious</u>

cau-<u>tious</u>   am-bi-<u>tious</u>   in-fec-<u>tious</u>
pre-ten-<u>tious</u>

9. eig ⎫
   eigh ⎭ Sound like <u>long a</u>:

b<u>eig</u>e   d<u>eig</u>n   f<u>eig</u>n   r<u>eig</u>n

<u>eig</u>ht   w<u>eigh</u>   n<u>eigh</u>-bor   fr<u>eigh</u>t

Once in a while <u>ei</u> will sound like long <u>a</u>: v<u>ei</u>n. But usually <u>ei</u> will have some other sound: s<u>ei</u>ze, s<u>ei</u>s-mo-graph, th<u>ei</u>r.

Once in a while <u>ey</u> will sound like long <u>a</u>: th<u>ey</u>. But usually <u>ey</u> will have some other sound: k<u>ey</u>, mon-<u>ey</u>.

10. er ⎫
    ir ⎬   Usually all three have the same sound:
    ur ⎭

h<u>er</u>	re-f<u>er</u>	p<u>er</u>-son	f<u>er</u>n
f<u>ir</u>	s<u>ir</u>	th<u>ir</u>-teen	d<u>ir</u>t
b<u>ur</u>	f<u>ur</u>	t<u>ur</u>-key	c<u>ur</u>l

SPECIAL CASES OF er, ir, AND ur
FOR ADVANCED STUDENTS

The <u>er</u> is in an accented syllable; another <u>r</u> comes right after <u>er</u>, and the <u>r</u> is at the beginning of the next syllable. The <u>er</u> usually will not use its team sound. Instead, the <u>e</u> usually will use its short <u>e</u> sound: <u>er</u>'-ror, m<u>er</u>'-ry, in-t<u>er</u>'-ro-gate'.

The <u>er</u> is in an accented syllable; a vowel comes right after <u>er</u>, and the vowel is at the beginning of the next syllable. The <u>er</u> usually will not use its team sound. Instead, the <u>e</u> usually will use its short <u>e</u> sound: v<u>er</u>'-y, k<u>er</u>'-o-sene', pros-p<u>er</u>'-i-ty.

The <u>er</u> is in an unaccented syllable. The <u>er</u> usually will sound like the <u>er</u> team said very fast and with very little force: p<u>er</u>-haps', af'-t<u>er</u>, en'-<u>er</u>-gy, gen'-<u>er</u>-ous.

Reminder to teachers: As you probably know, there is another situation that we did not include above: The <u>er</u> is in an unaccented syllable; another <u>r</u> comes right after <u>er</u>, and the <u>r</u> is at the beginning of the next syllable. When this happens, <u>er</u> might sound like a short <u>i</u>: <u>er</u>-rat'-ic; or the <u>er</u> might sound like a vowel often sounds in an unaccented syllable (a lot like a short <u>u</u> sound said very fast and with very little force): t<u>er</u>-rif'-ic.

Both cases are rare, especially the former. That is one reason we did not include this situation in the discussion for pupils. In addition, if a pupil does not recognize a word in which this situation occurs, he can attack that part of the word by using the clue in the paragraph that is just above this "Reminder to Teachers". That clue will not give the pupil the identical sound that the word uses, but the clue's sound should be close enough to enable the pupil to sound out that part of the word satisfactorily. So we could see no reason for burdening the pupil with this situation.

The ir is in an accented syllable or in an unaccented syllable; another r comes right after ir, and the r is at the beginning of the next syllable. The ir usually will not use its team sound. Instead, the i usually will use its short i sound: ir'-ri-gate; mir'-ror, ir-reg'-u-lar.

There is ir. A vowel comes right after ir, and the vowel is at the beginning of the next syllable. The ir usually will not use its team sound. Instead, the i usually will use its short i sound. (If ir has a vowel coming right after it, the ir syllable almost always will be accented. That is, this combination — ir + a vowel at the beginning of the next syllable — seems almost never to happen when ir is in an unaccented syllable): ir'-i-des'-cent, spir'-it, mir'-a-cle.

The ir is in an unaccented syllable. There are two main situations:

a. This situation already has been mentioned (in the first full paragraph on this page): There is ir in an unaccented syllable; there is another r right after the ir, and the r is at the beginning of the next syllable. The i usually will use its short i sound: ir-ra'-di-ate'.
b. There is ir in an unaccented syllable; the next syllable does not start with r. The ir usually will sound like the ir team said very fast and with very little force: cir-cum'-fer-ence, con'-fir-ma'-tion.

The ur is in an accented syllable; another r comes right after ur, and the r is at the beginning of the next syllable. A person usually will hear one of two things: The ur might sound like the ur team, or the u might sound like short u. (Whether a person hears the ur team sound or whether he hears the u making a short u sound seems to depend on how the person's talking and hearing have been trained): hur'-ry, cur'-rent, oc-cur'-rence.

The ur is in an accented syllable; a vowel comes right after ur, and the vowel is at the beginning of the next syllable. That word usually will be a derivative (that is, the word has been formed by adding an ending to a root word). The ur usually will not use its team sound. Instead, the u usually will keep the sound that it had in the root word. This sound usually will be either the long u sound or the sound of oo in moo: cure ➡ cur'-a-ble; as-sure' ➡ as-sur'-ance; en-dure' ➡ en-dur'-ance.

The ur is in an unaccented syllable. There are two main situations:

a. There is ur; there is another r right after the ur, and the r is at the beginning of the next syllable. A person usually will hear one of two things: The ur might sound like a short u sound said very fast and with very little force, or the ur might sound like the ur team said very fast and with very little force. (Which of the two a person hears seems to depend on how the person's talking and hearing have been trained): sur-round', cur-ric'-u-lum, in'-sur-rec'-tion.

b. There is ur in an unaccented syllable; the next syllable does not start with r. The ur usually will sound like the ur team said very fast and with very little force: sur-prise', meas'-ur-a-ble, in'-jure.

11A. ew   Sounds like long u:

few   pew   whew   neph-ew

11B. ew   Sounds like one of the oo team sounds — moo:

blew   chew   flew   grew

12. ion   will be at the end of the last syllable of a word or of a root word.

The ion team sounds a lot like yun said very fast and with very little force:

bun-ion   mil-lion   com-pan-ion   o-pin-ion

When ion comes right after s or t at the end of a word, ion loses its yun sound. That happens because the s or the t joins with the ion to form the sion or the tion vowel-consonant team. (See the sion and the tion vowel-consonant teams on pages 126-127, 127.)

13. ir   (See er, ir, ur.)

14. oi ⎫
    oy ⎬   They have the sound that I hear in these words:

oil	join	moist	point
oys-ter	boy	joy	toy

15A. oo   It has the sound that I hear in these words:

moo	cool	root	broom

15B. oo   It has the sound that I hear in these words:

good	hook	look	wool

The oo also might use the long vowel sound clue and make a long o sound: door, floor.

16. or   Sounds like the word or. (The o in or sounds like the sound of the au, aw teams):

or-der	for	sort	in-form

SPECIAL CASES OF or
FOR ADVANCED STUDENTS

The or is in an accented syllable; another r comes right after or, and the r is at the beginning of the next syllable. A person usually will hear one of two things: The or might sound like the or team, or the o might sound like short o. (Whether a person hears the or team sound, or whether he hears the o making a short o sound seems to depend on how the person's talking and hearing have been trained): sor'-ry, cor'-re-spond', to-mor'-row.

The or is in an accented syllable; a vowel comes right after or, and the vowel is at the beginning of the next syllable. A person usually will hear one of two things: The or might sound like the or team, or the o might sound like short o. (Whether a person hears the or team sound, or whether he hears the o making a short o sound seems to depend on how the person's talking and hearing have been trained): or'-i-gin, for'-est, his-tor'-ic.

There is w just before or in a one syllable word. The or often will sound like the er, ir, ur teams: word, worth, world.

In a word with more than one syllable: The w comes just before or in the same syllable; the syllable is accented. The or often will sound like the er, ir, ur teams: wor'-ship, wor'-thy, work'-er.

These two situations are not found in many words.

The or is in an unaccented syllable. There are two main situations:

a. There is or in the first syllable of a word; the first syllable is not accented. The or usually will sound like or: or-gan'-ic, for-ma'-tion, tor-na'-do.

b. There is or in an unaccented syllable; the or is not in the first syllable of the word. The or usually will sound like the er, ir, ur teams said very fast and with very little force: hon'-or, doc'-tor, mo'-tor-ize.

Reminder to teachers: As you probably know, there is another situation that we did not include in the discussion above. The situation is so rare. That is one reason we omitted the situation. In addition, if a pupil does not recognize a word in which this situation occurs, he can attack that part of the word by using clue a above. That clue will not give the pupil the identical sound that the word uses, but the clue a sound should enable the pupil to sound out that part of the word satisfactorily. So we could see no reason for burdening the pupil with this situation.

Here is the situation: The or is in an unaccented first syllable; another r is right after the or, and the r is at the beginning of the next syllable. In this situation, the or usually sounds like a vowel often sounds in an unaccented syllable (a lot like a short u sound said very fast and with very little force): cor-rect'.

17. ou ⎱
     ow ⎰

They make the sound that I might make if somebody pinched me:

out	mouth	sound	proud
owl	now	pow-der	crowd

The ou and the ow might also sound like long o: pour, own.

The ou sometimes might use the short u sound: rough.

The ou sometimes might borrow the sound of the au, aw teams: ought.

The ou sometimes might borrow an oo team sound: soup.

18. ous   will be at the end of the last syllable of a word or of a root word.

The ous team sounds a lot like us said very fast and with very little force:

joy-ous fa-mous nu-mer-ous tre-men-dous

19. ow   (See ou, ow.)

20. oy   (See oi, oy.)

21A. sion   will be at the end of the last syllable of a word or of a root word.

This sion team sounds a lot like shun said very fast and with very little force:

ex-pan-sion   per-mis-sion   pro-fes-sion

com-pre-hen-sion

21B. sion will be at the end of the last syllable of a word or of a root word.

The beginning sound of this sion team is a little bit different from the beginning sound of the sion team in 21A:

con-clu-sion   ex-cur-sion   in-va-sion

oc-ca-sion

22. sive will be at the end of the last syllable of a word or of a root word.

The sive team sounds like siv:

ag-gres-sive   ex-pen-sive   im-pul-sive

pos-ses-sive

This is really one of the regular exceptions to a long vowel sound clue (see exception number 2 on page 115). But this pattern of letters — sive — appears at or near the end of so many words that it is helpful to learn it as a team.

23. tial (See cial, tial.)

24. tion will be at the end of the last syllable of a word or of a root word.

The tion team sounds a lot like shun said very fast and with very little force:

ac-tion   mo-tion   na-tion   per-fec-tion

25. tious (See cious, tious.)

26. tive will be at the end of the last syllable of a word or of a root word.

The tive team sounds like tiv:

ac-tive at-ten-tive cre-a-tive in-struc-tive

This is really one of the regular exceptions to a long vowel sound clue (see exception number 2 on page 115). But this pattern of letters — tive — appears at or near the end of so many words that it is helpful to learn it as a team.

27. ture will be at the end of the last syllable of a word or of a root word.

The ture very often is a team that sounds a lot like chur said very fast and with very little force:

crea-ture   fu-ture   na-ture   ad-ven-ture

28. ur (See er, ir, ur.)

Minor Teams

We call these teams the minor teams, because they are not used as much as the major teams are.

1. al The a sounds like the sound of the au, aw teams (see Major Team 4). So the al team sounds like the word all:

al-so   halt

The a is especially likely to make this sound if ll comes right after the a: fall.

Notice that sometimes the l is silent: chalk.

Caution: Many times, al will not work as a team. Instead, the a in al might make some other sound: bale, calf.

2. alm The a sounds like a in the ar team (see Major Team 2). The l is silent. So the alm team sounds like this:

calm   palm

3. cient } will be at the end of the last syllable of a word
    tient } or of a root word.

> They sound a lot like <u>shint</u> or <u>shunt</u> said very
> fast and with very little <u>force</u>:

>> an-<u>cient</u>   suf-fi-<u>cient</u>
>>
>> pa-<u>tient</u>   quo-<u>tient</u>

4. gue   will be at the end of the last syllable of a word
              or of a root word.

> The <u>gue</u> team sounds like <u>hard g</u> (as in the
> word <u>go</u>):

>> lea<u>gue</u>   mon-o-lo<u>gue</u>

> Notice that <u>i</u> just before <u>gue</u> sounds like
> long <u>e</u>: fa-<u>tigue</u>.

5. ine   will be at the end of the last syllable of a word
              or of a root word.

> The <u>ine</u> team sounds like <u>ene</u>:

>> gas-o-l<u>ine</u>   mag-a-z<u>ine</u>

> **Caution:** Many times, <u>ine</u> will not work as
> a team. Instead, the <u>i</u> in <u>ine</u> might make a long
> i sound: tw<u>ine</u>; or a short <u>i</u> sound: mas-cu-
> l<u>ine</u>.

> Sometimes the <u>i</u> in other letter groups
> similar to <u>ine</u> might use the long <u>e</u> sound:
> au-to-mo-b<u>ile</u>, po-l<u>ice</u>.

6. que   will be at the end of the last syllable of a word
              or of a root word.

> The <u>que</u> team sounds like <u>k</u>:

>> pla<u>que</u>   pic-tur-es<u>que</u>

Notice that i just before que sounds like long e: an-tique.

7. tient   (See cient, tient.)

VOWELS IN UNACCENTED SYLLABLES

(If information about syllables is needed, see "What Is a Syllable?" on pages 167-168.)

(If information about accent is needed, see "Accented Syllables and Unaccented Syllables", starting on page 174.)

A one-syllable word might use a long vowel sound: ate (the clue is working), old (a regular exception); or a one-syllable word might use a short vowel sound: at (the clue is working), since (a regular exception).

The accented syllable of a longer word might use a long vowel sound: rea'-son (the clue is working), dan'-ger (a regular exception); or the accented syllable of a longer word might use a short vowel sound: en'-ter (the clue is working), ad-di'-tion (a regular exception).

An unaccented syllable of a longer word might use a long vowel sound: ro-ta'-tion (the clue is working); or an unaccented syllable of a longer word might use a short vowel sound: ac'-cent (the clue is working), mis'-chief (a regular exception).

But very often an unaccented syllable will not use a long vowel sound or a short vowel sound: ca-nal', can'-cel. Here are two reasons why that is true: 1) Often we say an unaccented syllable so fast that the vowel does not have time to give the sound that we expect it to give. 2) Often we do not say the unaccented syllable hard enough to force the vowel to give the sound that we expect it to give.

What is this sound that a vowel very often uses in a syllable that is not accented?

Strange as it may seem, all vowels sound very much alike in many unaccented syllables. This sound is a lot like a short u sound said very fast and with very little force.

Here are examples of that sound:

a   is making that sound: a-way', stan'-za

e   is making that sound: bro'-ken, si'-lent (sometimes e

in an unaccented syllable sounds
like short i: bas'-ket)

i   is making that sound: pen'-cil, pu'-pil

o   is making that sound: ba'-con, per'-son

u   is making that sound: cir'-cus, mi'-nus

Now, how do accented syllables and unaccented syllables affect the vowel sound teams and the vowel-consonant teams?

First, let's consider the teams that belong at the end of the last syllable of a word or of a root word. I should give these teams their team sound whether the syllable is accented or not. (Just remember the caution for ine. The letters ine very often do not work as a team whether the syllable is accented or not.)

Ar; er, ir, ur; and or in accented syllables and in unaccented syllables were discussed on pages 118-119, 121-123, and 124-126. They usually use their team sounds in one-syllable words and in the accented syllables of longer words, except for the special cases which were described in the "Special Cases" explanations. The sounds that they usually make in unaccented syllables also were described in the "Special Cases" explanations.

The other teams usually appear only in one-syllable words or in accented syllables of longer words. Usually we will not see them in unaccented syllables at all. When one of these teams does show up in an unaccented syllable, it usually will use its team sound anyway: neph'-ew, foun-da'-tion. Once in a while, however, a team might not use its team sound in an unaccented syllable: cam'-ou-flage. (In that word, ou sounds like any vowel might sound in an unaccented syllable — like a short u sound said very fast and with very little force.)

SUMMARY OF VOWEL SOUNDS

Here we have a summary of the sounds that vowels will use.

In the list below, we will show the sounds that belong to each vowel. We must be sure to remember, though, that a vowel might borrow the sound of some other vowel. The vowel might use the borrowed sound instead of its own sound in some particular word. We will see many examples of how that is done when we study the Freaks in the next section of this book. (For example, think about the word son. In this word, o does not use any of its own sounds. Instead, o borrows and uses the short sound of u. Also consider the word com-pan-ion. The i is not using any of its own sounds. In fact, the i is not using any vowel sound. Instead, i is using the consonant sound of y).

Here are the sounds that belong to each vowel:

a:
long a: ate

short a: at

a in the alm team ⎱ ⎰ palm
a in the ar team ⎰ ⎱ arm

a in the are team: share

a in the al team ⎱ ⎰ malt   (This sound also
au, aw teams ⎰ ⎱ au-tumn, draw   belongs to o in
                                   the or team.)

e:
long e: eat

short e: echo

er team: her   (This sound also belongs to the
                    ir team and to the ur team.)

i:
long i: I'm

short i̱:   in̲

i̲r team: sti̱r   (This sound also belongs to the
                                er team and to the u̲r team.)

O:
long o̲:   go̲

short o̲:   o̲x

o̲ in the o̲r team: o̲r   (This sound also belongs to a̲
                                in the a̲l team and to the au̲,
                                aw teams.)

o̲i, o̲y teams: o̲il, bo̲y

o̲o team 1:   mo̲o

o̲o team 2:   bo̲ok

o̲u, o̲w teams: o̲ut, o̲wl

u:
long u̲:   u̲se

short u̲:   u̲s

u̲r team: fu̲r   (This sound also belongs to the
                                er team and to the i̲r team.)

Here is the sound that vowels often make in syllables
that are not accented (the sound is a lot like a short u̲ sound
said very fast and with very little force):

a: a̲-go'

e: bro'-ke̲n   or like short i̲:   bas'-ke̲t

i: pu'-pi̲l

o: ba'-co̲n

u: cir'-cu̲s

SECTION 16

FREAKS — MORE ABOUT EXCEPTIONS

Sometimes the way a word (or part of a word) sounds is entirely different from the way we expect it to sound. No clue that we have studied seems to fit this word (or this part of the word). For that reason, it often is impossible to sound out such a word. Words like that really are freaks.

Suppose that I don't recognize a word. I try to figure it out (see Section 18, suggestions 1-11 on pages 184-186), but I can't. There is a good chance that the word is one of those freaks. If I can't figure out the word, I should use the dictionary. Then I should notice what the word (especially the freaky part of the word) looks like and what it sounds like. I should remember that, so when I see the word again, I will recognize the freak, and I won't be stumped all over again.

Here are some of those words:

a-gainst	The ai sounds like short e.
an-swer	The w is silent.
an-y	The a sounds like short e.
blood	The oo sounds like short u.
colo-nel	The olo sounds like er.
come	The ome sounds like um.
could	The oul sounds like the oo team in cook.
does	The oe sounds like short u.
earth	The ear sounds like the er team.
eye	The whole word sounds like long i.
fa-ther	The a sounds like a in the ar team.
hon-est	The h is silent.
is-land	The s is silent.
love	The ove sounds like uv.
moth-er	The o sounds like short u.

move	The o sounds like the oo team in moo. The e is silent.
one	The whole word sounds like wun.
put	The u sounds like the oo team in foot.
re-ceipt	The p is silent.
recipe	The word should be divided like this: re-cipe; in the last syllable, the i should be long, and the e should be silent. Instead, the word is divided like this: rec-i-pe; the e is not silent.
rule	The u sounds like the oo team in moo.
sew	The ew sounds like long o.
shoe	The oe sounds like the oo team in moo.
ski	The i sounds like long e.
swat	The a sounds like short o.
through	The ough sounds like the oo team in moo.
two	The wo sounds like the oo team in moo.
who	The w is silent. The o sounds like the oo team in moo.

Another kind of freak is like a vowel-consonant team. The trouble is that each letter combination is used too seldom to be regarded as a real team. So we regard them as a kind of freak.

cli'-mate	The ate usually will sound like ate should sound, but sometimes ate will sound like it.
gar-de'-nia	The i sounds like consonant y. The a has the sound that a vowel often has in an unaccented syllable.
gen'-ial	The i sounds like consonant y. The a has the sound that a vowel often has in an unaccented syllable.
ci-vil'-ian	The i sounds like consonant y. The a has the sound that a vowel often has in an unaccented syllable.

fa-mil'-iar	The i sounds like consonant y. The ar sounds like the er, ir, ur teams said very fast and with very little force.
al'-ien	The i sounds like consonant y. The e has the sound that a vowel often has in an unaccented syllable.
con-ven'-ience	The i sounds like consonant y. The e has the sound that a vowel often has in an unaccented syllable.
con-ven'-ient	The i sounds like consonant y. The e has the sound that a vowel often has in an unaccented syllable.
jun'-ior	The i sounds like consonant y. The or sounds like the er, ir, ur teams said very fast and with very little force.
gen'-ius	The i sounds like consonant y. The u has the sound that a vowel often has in an unaccented syllable.

As we can see, the i is using the consonant sound of y. The i does that sometimes when it starts the last syllable of a word.

Here is the last kind of freak that we will examine. These words came to us from the French language. The sounds which certain letter groups make are different from the sounds that we expect those letter groups to make. So in our language they are freaks.

ca-fe'	The e' sounds like our long a.
bu-reau	The eau sounds like our long o.
bal-let	The et sounds like our long a.
mi-gnon	The gn sounds like ny.

SECTION 17

WORDS AND PARTS OF WORDS

Compound Words

Prefix, Root Word, Suffix
> Let's Continue with Prefixes
> Let's Continue with Suffixes

Root Words That Change

More about Prefixes, Roots, and Suffixes
> Making English Words from Latin Roots
> Making English Words from Greek Roots

What Is a Syllable?

How Can I Divide a Word into Syllables?
> Clues for Dividing a Word into Syllables

Accented Syllables and Unaccented Syllables
> Patterns of Accent
> Clues for Accenting Syllables

COMPOUND WORDS

A compound word was made by putting two or more words together to make one bigger word.

The meaning of the compound word might be the meaning of one of the words plus the meaning of the other word or words. (For example, sand and hill make sandhill. Sandhill means a hill of sand.) Or the meaning of the new word might be just suggested by the meaning of each word that makes up the compound word. (For example, air and port make airport. An airport is not a port for air or a port in the air. But an airport is a port for airplanes — a place where airplanes can load and unload.)

Each word in a real compound word will sound the same in the compound word as it does by itself outside the compound word.

Here are some examples of compound words:

air	and	port	to make	airport
corn	and	field	to make	cornfield
fire	and	place	to make	fireplace
head	and	quarters	to make	headquarters
lime	and	stone	to make	limestone
moon	and	light	to make	moonlight
news	and	paper	to make	newspaper
oat	and	meal	to make	oatmeal
play	and	mate	to make	playmate
stage	and	coach	to make	stagecoach
stream	and	line	to make	streamline
view	and	point	to make	viewpoint
ware	and	house	to make	warehouse
year	and	book	to make	yearbook

never	and	the	and	less	to make	nevertheless
now	and	a	and	days	to make	nowadays

PREFIX, ROOT WORD, SUFFIX

Knowing about prefixes and suffixes will help me in three main ways:

Knowing about prefixes and suffixes will help me to recognize many words more easily and more quickly.

Knowing about prefixes and suffixes will help me to figure out many words that I do not recognize at first.

Knowing about prefixes and suffixes will help me to get a clearer understanding of the meaning of many words.

Now, what are prefixes, root words, and suffixes?

A prefix is a letter or a group of letters put at the be- ginning of a real word in order to change the meaning of the word or to make a new word.

A suffix is also called an ending. A suffix is a letter or a group of letters put at the end of a real word in order to change the meaning of the word or to make a new word.

A root word is also called a base word. Or a root word might be called a root. A root word is the word that a pre- fix or a suffix has been attached to.

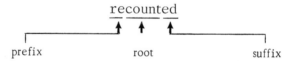

I know that count means to find out how much or how many. When I put the prefix re on the front of count, I get the word recount. This means to count again.

When I put the suffix ed on the end of count, I get the word counted. Counted means that the counting already has been done — the counting was done in the past (past tense). When I put the suffix ed on the end of recount, I get the word recounted. Recounted means that the recounting already has been done — the recounting was done in the past (past tense).

The prefix re also might bring another meaning to the root word. For example, repay does not mean to pay again. It means to pay back. So we see that a prefix might have more than one meaning.

Let's Continue with Prefixes

Here are some more prefixes with examples of how they work:

dislike . . . . the opposite of like

interstate . . . . between states
or
among states

interweave . . . . weave together

intracity competition. . . . . competition within a city

miscount. . . . . count wrongly
or
a wrong count

misfit. . . . . fit badly
or
a bad fit

postgame . . . . after the game

pregame. . . . . before the game

transatlantic . . . . across the Atlantic
or
on the other side of the Atlantic
or
over the Atlantic

transpierce. . . . . pierce through

unhappy . . . . not happy

unlock . . . . the opposite of lock

Here are more prefixes with many of their meanings:

(We hope that the information in parenthesis — ( ) — will make it easier to understand the meaning of the example that we have used.)

(*Caution:* The student should ignore information in brackets — [ ] — at this time. That information might con-

142

fuse a student until he thoroughly understands the information in "Making English Words from Latin Roots," which starts on page 161.)

a	in	abed
	in the act of (root word + ing)	asleep
	on	afoot
	to (the)	ashore
a	see also [ ] after ab	
a	see also [ ] after ad	
a	see also [an]	
ab	away, away from, departing from, from, off, outside of . . .	abnormal
	[It also might appear as a with roots that usually are not regular English words: avert.]	
ac	see [ ] after ad	
ad	to, toward	adjoin
	[It also might appear as a, ac, af, ag, al, an, ap, ar, as, or at with roots that usually are not regular English words: ascend, accept, affect, aggressive, alloy, announce, applaud, arrive, assist, attach.]	
af	see [ ] after ad	
ag	see [ ] after ad	
al	see [ ] after ad	
an	not, without	anarchy
	It is used with roots that usually are not regular English words.	
	It also might appear as a: apathy.	
an	see also [ ] after ad	
ant	see anti	
ante	before.	antedate
anti	act(s) against, prevent(s)	antifreeze
	against, opposed to	antislavery
	not, the opposite of	antisocial
	It also might appear as ant: antacid.	
ap	see [ ] after ad	
ar	see [ ] after ad	

arch	chief, first, main, most important	archenemy
	[This should not be confused with the <u>arch</u> in <u>archaeology</u>. The word <u>archaeology</u> begins with a word element <u>archaeo</u>, which means <u>ancient</u>, <u>primitive</u>.]	
	[<u>arch</u> also might appear as <u>archi</u> with roots that usually are not regular English words: <u>architect</u>.]	
as	see [ ] after <u>ad</u>	
at	see [ ] after <u>ad</u>	
auto	self, of oneself	<u>auto</u>biography
	(root word) to oneself	<u>auto</u>suggestion
be	about, against, at, for, on	<u>be</u>wail
	all around, all over, thoroughly	<u>be</u>sprinkle
	cause to seem, make	<u>be</u>calm
	provide with (<u>a</u>)	<u>be</u>friend
bi	doubly, has two (root word + s),	
	two (root word + s)	<u>bi</u>fold
	every second (root word without ly ending),	
	once every two (root word without ly ending, + s)	<u>bi</u>weekly
	twice (<u>a</u> + root word without ly ending)	<u>bi</u>weekly
by	less important, minor	<u>by</u>-road
	near, near by	<u>by</u>-stander
circum	about, around, in a circle, on all sides	<u>circum</u>navigate
co	equally	<u>co</u>extend
	jointly, together, with	<u>co</u>exist
col	see [ ] after <u>com</u>	
com	altogether, jointly, together, with	<u>com</u>press
	[It also might appear as <u>col</u>, <u>con</u>, or <u>cor</u> with roots that usually are not regular English words: <u>col</u>lide, <u>con</u>nect, <u>cor</u>rect.]	
con	see [ ] after <u>com</u>	
contra	against, in opposition, opposite	<u>contra</u>position
cor	see [ ] after <u>com</u>	
counter	against, in opposition to, (<u>an</u>) opposing (root word)	<u>counter</u>act
	corresponding (meaning <u>alike</u> or <u>similar</u>)	<u>counter</u>part
	in return	<u>counter</u>attack
	opposite of	<u>counter</u>clockwise
de	away, away from, from	<u>de</u>part
	completely, entirely	<u>de</u>spoil
	down	<u>de</u>press
	get off (<u>the</u>)	<u>de</u>train
	make lower (<u>the</u>), reduce (<u>the</u>)	<u>de</u>value

de (continued)

	off (the).	derail
	remove (the)	dehair
	remove from (the)	dethrone
	reverse (the action of the root word), the opposite of. . . .	decode
di	(has) double (root word without ic ending, + s), (has) two (root word without ic ending, + s).	diatomic
di	see also [ ] after dis	
dif	see [ ] after dis	
dis	opposite of.	dislike

[It also might mean apart, away and also might appear
as di or dif with roots that usually are not regular English
words: dispel, divert, differ.]

e	see [ ] after ex	
ec	see [ ] after ex	
ef	see [ ] after ex	
em	cause to be, make.	embitter
	in, put in.	empower
en	cause to be, make.	endear
	in (a), put in (a), put into (a)	encircle
	put on (a).	enthrone

ep —⟩ among, at, on, to ⟨	epoch
epi —⟩	epidermis

They are used with roots that usually are not regular
English words.

ex	former, formerly	ex-president
	away, from, out, out of.	express

[It also might mean completely, thoroughly when used
with roots that usually are not regular English words:
exuberant.]

[It also might appear as e, ec, or ef, meaning away,
from, out, out of, with roots that usually are not regular
English words: erupt, eczema, effect.]

extra	besides, beyond, outside.	extraordinary

[It also might appear as extro with roots that usually are
not regular English words: extrovert.]

extro	see [ ] after extra	
fore	ahead (of), before	forenoon
	beforehand.	foretell

fore (continued)

   front, at the front (of the), in front (of the), near the
   front (of the) . . . .   forebrain
   main. . . . .   foreman

hemi half . . . .   hemisphere

hydr see [   ] after hydro

hydro having to do with water, of water . . . .   hydroplane
   combined with hydrogen.   hydrocarbon
   [It also might appear as hydr with roots that usually are
  not regular English words: hydraulic.]

hyper above (the usual amount of), beyond (the usual amount of).   hyperacidity
   exceedingly, over, to excess, too, very . . . .   hypersensitive

hypo below (the usual amount of), beneath (the usual amount of),
   in a lesser degree (of), less (root word without ity ending),
   less than (the usual amount of), slightly (root word without
   ity ending), somewhat (root word without ity ending),
   under (the usual amount of).   hypoacidity

il   in, into, inward, on, toward, upon, within. . . . .   illapse
   not, the absence of (root word + ity), the opposite of . . . .   illegal

im   in, into, inward, on, toward, upon, within. . . . .   impress
   put in, put into . . . .   imprison
   not, the absence of (root word without e + ity), the
   opposite of. . . . .   impure

in   in, into, inward, on, toward, upon, within. . . . .   ingrown
   put in (a), put into (a). . . . .   incase
   not, the absence of (root word without e + ity), the
   opposite of. . . . .   inactive

inter See the list on page 141.

intra See the list on page 141.

intro in, into, inwardly, within . . . .   introspection
   It is used with roots that usually are not regular English
  words.

ir   in, into, on, upon. . . . .   irradiate
   not, the absence of (root word + ity), the opposite of . . . .   irregular

mal bad, faulty, poor. . . . .   maladjustment
   badly, poorly . . . .   maladjusted

mid at the middle of, in the middle of, middle of, near the
   middle of, of the middle of . . . .   midday

mis See the list on page 141.

mon see [   ] after mono

mono	(a + root word) alone, one, single.................	monorail
	[It also might appear as mon: monatomic.]	
multi	has many (root word without ed, + s), has several (root word without ed, + s), many	multicolored
non	failure to be, not, opposite of	noncivilized
	lack of	nonpayment
	without	nonprofit
o	see [ob]	

ob against, on, over, to, toward.................. observe
It is used with roots that usually are not regular English words.
It also might appear as o, oc, of, op, or os with roots that usually are not regular English words: omit, occlude, offer, opponent, ostensible.

oc	see [ob]	
of	see [ob]	
op	see [ob]	
os	see [ob]	
out	at a distance, distant, beyond, outside.............	outfield
	forth	outburst
	better than...............................	outplay
	longer than	outlast
	more than	outsell
	out, outward.............................	outflow
over	extra	overtime
	over...................................	overflow
	too, very................................	overcrowded
	too much................................	overeat
	too long................................	oversleep
pan	all	Pan-American

par } { beside, by, near; amiss; aside, beyond; } { parish
para } { against, contrary to; guard against, ward off } { parasol
They are used with roots that usually are not regular English words.

per completely, thoroughly, very; through .... perfect
It is used with roots that usually are not regular English words.

peri	around, near	perimeter
	It is used with roots that usually are not regular English words.	
poly	many (root word without ic, + s), more than one (root word without ic), several (root word without ic, + s)	polyatomic
	much, very	poly-unsaturated
post	See the list on page 141.	
pre	See the list on page 141.	
pro	for (the), in favor of (the).	pro-British
	for (a), in place of (a)	pronoun
	[It also might mean before, forth, forward when used with roots that usually are not regular English words: prologue, proceed.]	
quadr quadri—four quadru	. . . .	quadrangle quadrilateral quadruped
	They are used with roots that usually are not regular English words.	
re	again, once more	recount
	back.	repay
retro	back, backward, behind	retrospect
	It is used with roots that usually are not regular English words.	
se	apart, aside, without	select
	It is used with roots that usually are not regular English words.	
self	automatic, automatically	self-winding
	by oneself	self-made
	for oneself.	self-respect
	in oneself	self-confidence
	of oneself	self-conscious
	on oneself	self-imposed
	over oneself.	self-control
	to oneself	self-addressed
semi	half	semicircle
	incompletely, partly	semiskilled
	twice (a + root word without ly ending)	semimonthly
sub	again, further.	subdivide
	(the + root word) below, (the + root word) down, (the + root word) under.	subsoil

sub (continued)

	in a lesser degree, moderately, slightly, somewhat.	subacid
	in a lower position, in an inferior position, in a lesser position, of less importance	subtitle
	near (the + root word without al ending, + s), nearly	subtropical

[It also might appear as suc, suf, sug, sum, sup, sur, or sus with roots that usually are not regular English words: succumb, suffer, suggest, summon, supply, surreptitious, suspend.]

suc	see [ ] after sub
suf	see [ ] after sub
sug	see [ ] after sub
sum	see [ ] after sub
sup	see [ ] after sub

super	above, over	superstructure
	besides (the normal), in addition to (the normal).	supertax
	beyond (what is), more than, surpassing (what is)	superhuman
	exceedingly, in high proportion, to excess, to a great degree, very	superacid

sur	above, up.	surmount
	beyond	surpass
	exceedingly, (an) excessive, too much.	surcharge
	over.	surprint

sur	see also [ ] after sub
sus	see [ ] after sub

syl		syllable
sym	together, with	sympathy
syn		synonym

They are used with roots that usually are not regular English words.

tetra	four	tetrahedron

It is used with roots that usually are not regular English words.

trans	See the list on page 141.

tri	every third (root word without ly ending), once every three (root word without ly ending, + s).	triweekly
	has three (root word + s)	tricolor
	three	trifold
	three times (a + root word without ly ending).	triweekly
ultra	beyond (the).	ultraviolet

ultra (continued)

exceedingly, excessively, extremely, more (root word)
than what is usual, very, (has) excessive (root word + y) .   ultramodest

un   See the list on page 141.

under   below, beneath (the), lower (than the), under (the)...... underground
below normal, less than the usual .... underage
less than................................ underbid
lower than................................ undersell ·
lower in rank.............................. undersecretary
not enough, too little .... underpay

uni   one, single................................ unicolor

Let's Continue with Suffixes

A suffix might change the meaning of the root word in different ways.

We already have seen that the suffix ed changes the meaning of a root word that is a verb by changing the time (tense) when the action of the root word takes place (page 140). Let's consider one more example of that: When the word climb is used, the action takes place now — in the present (present tense). But when the word climbed is used, we know that the action already has taken place — in the past (past tense).

A suffix might change the meaning of a root word by changing the root word's part of speech. (The parts of speech are noun, pronoun, adjective, verb, adverb, conjunction, preposition, and interjection.) Changing the root word's part of speech changes the way in which the meaning of the root word will be used. For example, the suffix ly might change a noun to an adjective: man ➡ manly (like a man). Or the suffix ly might change an adjective to an adverb: brave ➡ bravely (in a brave way). Artist is a noun, but artistic is an adjective and might mean of an artist or like an artist. Digest usually is a verb, but digestible is an adjective and might mean can be digested. Sometimes the adding of a suffix to a root word changes the way in which the meaning of the root word is used more than it changes the actual meaning of the root word itself. This is true of the examples that we have just seen. Other times, however, the meaning of the root word is changed a lot. For example, hope might be a noun. If we add the suffix less, we get the new word hopeless, which is an adjective. This time, we have changed the root word's part of speech, and we have changed the root word's meaning a great deal, too. This is true, because hopeless means without hope.

A suffix might change the meaning of the root word without changing its tense or its part of speech. Let's take the word book, a noun. Now we will add the suffix let (which might mean little). We get a new word booklet. Booklet, which means a little book, also is a noun. So there has been no change in the part of speech. Since book and booklet are nouns, they have no tense, so there has been no change of tense. Only the meaning of the root word has been changed, and that has been changed a lot.

Here are some more suffixes with examples of how they work:

baked. . . . . the past tense of bake

lifted . . . . the past tense of lift

honeyed . . . . . . like honey

moneyed. . . . . . has money

worker. . . . . . . a person who works
or
a thing that works

highlander . . . . a person who lives in the highlands

faster . . . . more fast

fastest . . . . most fast

foxes . . . . more than one fox

teaches . . . . . . It, he, she teaches. I, you, we, they teach.

hopeful. . . . . . . full of hope

hopeless. . . . . . without hope

countless . . . . . cannot be counted

books. . . . . more than one book

climbs. . . . . . . It, he, she climbs. I, you, we, they climb.

Here are more suffixes with many of their meanings:

able	able to be (root word + ed), can be (root word + ed).	washable
	can (root word), inclined to (root word), might (root word)	perishable
	deserves to be (root word + ed).	punishable
	likely to (root word), suitable for (root word).	comfortable
age	act of (root word + ing)	spoilage
	action of a (root word).	leverage
	collection of (root word + s), group of (root word + s) . . . . (bag + age) =	baggage
	condition of (root word), rank of (root word)	peerage
	cost of (root word + s), fee for (root word + s), payment for (a + root word)	mileage
	home of (root word + s), residence of (root word + s) . . .	orphanage
	total number of (root word + s)	mileage
al	act of (root word + ing) . . . . (refuse + al) =	refusal
	like (a + root word), of (a + root word), related to (a + root word).	verbal
an	having to do with (root word), related to (root word) . . . . (Mexico + an) =	Mexican
	belongs to (root word), of (root word).	Mexican
	inhabitant of (root word), native of (root word).	Mexican
ance	act of (root word + ing)	attendance
	state of being (root word + ed).	annoyance
ant	a person who (root word + s), a thing that (root word + s)	informant
	(root word + ing). . . . . (please + ant) =	pleasant
ar	a person who (root word + s), a thing that (root word + s) . . . . (beg + ar) =	beggar
	like (a + root word), of (a + root word), related to (a + root word), refers to (a + root word)	linear
arium	a collection of (root word + s), a place for (root word + s), related to (root word + s).	insectarium
ary	being (root word), has the nature of (root word)	secondary
	characterized by (root word), related to (root word)	customary
	collection of (root word + s) . . . . (statue + ary) =	statuary
	having to do with (a + root word), of (a + root word)	missionary
	person who (has + root word + s).	visionary
	place for (the + root word)	infirmary

152

ary (continued)

thing that (root word + s) . . . .   boundary

ate   cause to be (root word), make (root word) . . . .   domesticate
concerned with (a + root word), having to do with (a +
root word), like (a + root word), of (a + root word)
. . . . (college + ate) =   collegiate
contains (root word), has (root word) . . . .   affectionate
duties of (root word), office of (root word), position of
(root word) . . . .   consulate
mix with (root word), supply with (root word), treat with
(root word) . . . . (chlorine + ate) =   chlorinate
salt formed from (root word + ic) acid . . . .   carbonate

ation   act of (root word + ing), state of (root word + ing). . . . . .   taxation
result of (root word + ing) . . . . (civilize + ation) =   civilization
state of being (root word + ed). . . . . . (examine + ation) =   examination

ative   concerned with (root word + ing), has the power to (root
word), related to (root word + ing) . . . . .(cause + ative) =   causative
inclined to (root word), likely to (root word) . . . .   talkative

cide   killer of (root word + s) . . . . (insect + cide) =   insecticide
killing of (root word + s) . . . . (insect + cide) =   insecticide

cy   (root word) condition, fact of being (root word), (root
word) state . . . .   normalcy
office of (root word), position of (root word)
. . . . . . (president + cy) =   presidency
rank of (root word) . . . .(lieutenant + cy) =   lieutenancy

d   See the list on page 150.

dom   all who are (root word + s) . . . .   officialdom
condition of being (root word), state of being (root word) .   freedom
position of (a + root word), rank of (a + root word),
region of (a + root word) . . . .   princedom

ed   See the list on page 150.

ee   person who is (root word). . . . .   absentee
person who is (root word + ed) . . . .   employee
(Notice that we have the meaning for ee listed twice. We
have done that to illustrate how sometimes it is necessary to
change what we are thinking a little bit in order to make the
same meaning fit different words. We shall do this again
from time to time as a reminder.)

eer   person who works with (root word + s) . . . .   auctioneer
person who is concerned with (root word + s). . . . .   auctioneer

en   become (root word). . . . .   weaken

en (continued)

	cause (<u>something</u>) to be (root word), make (<u>something</u> + root word)................................	weaken
	cause (<u>something</u>) to have (root word).............	strengthen
	like (root word)	golden
	made of (root word).........................	golden
	more than one (root word)	oxen
	the past participle of (root word)................	eaten
ence	act of (root word + ing), state of (root word + ing)......	dependence
	state of being (root word + ent)	dependence
ency	act of (root word + ing), state of (root word + ing)......	dependency
	state of being (root word + ent)	dependency
ent	a person who (root word + s), a thing that (root word + s).................................	dependent
	(root word + ing)...........................	dependent
er	See the list on page 150.	
ery	act of (root word + ing)	mockery
	actions of (<u>a</u> + root word).....................	foolery
	being (<u>a</u> + root word), qualities of (<u>a</u> + root word) ....(snob + ery) =	snobbery
	business of (<u>a</u> + root word), occupation of (<u>a</u> + root word)......................................	cookery
	business of (root word + ing), occupation of (root word + ing)..................................	cookery
	place for (root word + ing) ....(can + ery) =	cannery
	place for (root word + s)	fernery
	use of (root word + s)	trickery
es	See the list on page 150.	
ese	belongs to (root word), of (root word).............	Japanese
	having to do with (root word), related to (root word)	Japanese
	language of (root word)	Japanese
	native of (root word)	Japanese
esque	in the (root word) manner, in the (root word) style	Romanesque
	like a (root word) ....(picture + esque) =	picturesque
ess	female (root word)	lioness
est	See the list on page 150.	
ette	female (root word)	drum majorette
	imitation (root word), substitute (root word)	leatherette
	little (root word)...........................	kitchenette
ey	full of (root word)..........................	clayey
	contains (root word)	clayey

ey (continued)

      like (root word) .... clay<u>ey</u>

      of (root word). .... clay<u>ey</u>

fold   divided into (root word) parts, has (root word) parts.... two<u>fold</u>

      (root word) times as great, (root word) times as many,

      (root word) times as much .... two<u>fold</u>

ful   See the list on page 150.

fy   become (root word)......................... rare<u>fy</u>

      cause to be (root word), change into (<u>a</u> + root word +

      <u>condition</u>), make (root word).................... rare<u>fy</u>

hood   state of being (<u>a</u> + root word) .... boy<u>hood</u>

      (root word + s) as a group .... boy<u>hood</u>

ial   like (<u>an</u> + root word), of (<u>an</u> + root word)........... adverb<u>ial</u>

ian   belongs to (root word), of (root word).............. Charleston<u>ian</u>

      having to do with (root word), related to (root word) .... music<u>ian</u>

ible   able to be (root word + ed), can be (root word + ed)..... digest<u>ible</u>

ic   like (<u>an</u> + root word), of (<u>an</u> + root word), related to (<u>an</u>

      + root word)............................ artist<u>ic</u>

      being (root word), contains (root word), is made of (root

      word) ....(metal + ic) = metall<u>ic</u>

ie   little (root word); (also used to show affection) .... dear<u>ie</u>

ier   person who works with (root word + s), person who is

      concerned with (root word + s) .... cloth<u>ier</u>

ify   become (root word)......................... solid<u>ify</u>

      cause to be (root word), change into (root word), make

      (root word) .... solid<u>ify</u>

ine   like (<u>an</u> + root word), of (root word + s) .... elephant<u>ine</u>

      made of (root word + s) ....(crystal + ine) = crystall<u>ine</u>

ing   action of the verb (root word) .... draw<u>ing</u>

      material for (root word + s) .... sheet<u>ing</u>

      (<u>profession</u>) of a person who (root word + es)......... teach<u>ing</u>
                                      profession

      present participle of (root word) .... fall<u>ing</u>

      (<u>a</u>) product of the verb (root word), (<u>a</u>) result of the verb

      (root word) .... a draw<u>ing</u>

      (<u>a star</u>) that (root word + s), (<u>a star</u>) who (root word

      + s) ....(rise + ing) = a ris<u>ing</u> star

      using (<u>a</u> + root word), using (root word + s).......... boat<u>ing</u>

ion   act of (root word + ing), state of (root word + ing)

                             ..... (commune + ion) = commun<u>ion</u>

      result of (root word + ing), thing (root word + ed)...... invent<u>ion</u>

      state of being (root word + ed).................... oppres<u>sion</u>

ish	a little more than (root word)	twentyish
	belongs to (the + root word + s), of (the + root word + s) . . . . (Dane + ish) =	Danish
	having to do with (the + root word + s), related to (the + root word + s) . . . . (Dane + ish) =	Danish
	like (a + root word).	boyish
	somewhat (root word)	brownish
ism	action or actions of (a + root word), quality or qualities of (a + root word).	heroism
	(root word) belief, (root word) practice, (root word) principle.	humanitarianism
	(root word) characteristic, (root word) condition, (root word) state	Americanism
ist	person who (root word + s), person who takes (a + root word).	vacationist
	person who knows about (root word + s)	organist
	person who makes (root word + s), person who makes (a + root word).	tourist
ite	person associated with (root word).	laborite
itis	inflammation of (the + root word). . . . . . .(tonsil + itis) =	tonsillitis
ity	condition of being (root word), fact of being (root word), state of being (root word).	legality
	degree of being (root word), quality of being (root word) .	legality
ive	has the power to (root word), related to (root word + ing)	corrective
	has the nature of (root word).	excessive
	has the quality of (root word + ing).	corrective
	inclined to (root word), likely to (root word)	corrective
ize	become (root word), becomes (root word)	vaporize
	make (root word)	legalize
kin	little (root word).	lambkin
less	See the list on page 150.	
let	little (root word).	booklet
	object worn as a band on (the + root word).	armlet
like	like (root word), resembles (root word)	lifelike
	fit for (root word), right for (root word), suited to (root word)	businesslike
ling	belongs to (root word), concerned with (root word)	earthling
	little (root word), unimportant (root word), young (root word).	princeling
	person who is (root word), thing that is (root word).	weakling

ly	at a (root word) time...................................	recent<u>ly</u>
	for each (root word), of each (root word).............	hour<u>ly</u>
	in a (root word) way, to a (root word) degree.........	perfect<u>ly</u>
	like a (root word).....................................	man<u>ly</u>
ment	act of (root word + ing), fact of (root word + ing), state of (root word + ing)......................................	agree<u>ment</u>
	fact of being (root word + ed), state of being (root word + ed)..	conceal<u>ment</u>
	product of (root word + ing), result of (root word + ing)..	refine<u>ment</u>
most	more (root word without ther) than all others, most (root word without ther) of all...............................	farther<u>most</u>
ness	being (root word), quality of being (root word), state of being (root word).....................................	soft<u>ness</u>
oid	like (<u>a</u> + root word)................(cube + oid) =	cub<u>oid</u>
	thing like (<u>a</u> + root word)............(cube + oid) =	cub<u>oid</u>
or	person who (root word + s), thing that (root word + s)...	act<u>or</u>
ory	for the purpose of (root word + ing), having to do with (root word + ing)....................................	prohibit<u>ory</u>
	has the nature of (root word + ing)...................	contradict<u>ory</u>
	inclined to (root word), likely to (root word).........	contradict<u>ory</u>
	place for (root word + ing)...........................	deposit<u>ory</u>
	(root word + ing).....................................	contradict<u>ory</u>
	thing for the purpose of (root word + ing)............	direct<u>ory</u>
ous	full of (root word), has (root word), has a lot of (root word)..	courage<u>ous</u>
	has the nature of (root word), like (root word)........	thunder<u>ous</u>
	inclined to (root word), likely to (root word) ...... (infect + ous) =	infect<u>ious</u>
proof	protected against (root word), safe from (root word)....	frost<u>proof</u>
ry	act of (root word + ing), action of (root word + ing).....	rival<u>ry</u>
	act of (<u>a</u> + root word), action of (<u>a</u> + root word).......	rival<u>ry</u>
	act of (root word + s), action of (root word + s).......	rival<u>ry</u>
	collection of (root word + s), group of (root word + s)...	jewel<u>ry</u>
	work of (<u>a</u> + root word)...........................	dentist<u>ry</u>
	work of (root word + s)..............................	dentist<u>ry</u>
	(root word) condition, (root word) quality, (root word) state...	savage<u>ry</u>
s	See the list on pages 150-151.	
ship	being (root word + s)................................	friend<u>ship</u>
	office of (root word), rank of (root word)............	governor<u>ship</u>
	skill of (<u>a</u> + root word).........................	workman<u>ship</u>
	state of being (<u>a</u> + root word)	citizen<u>ship</u>

sion	act of (root word + ing), state of (root word + ing)	
	. . . . (divide + sion) =	divi<u>sion</u>
	result of (root word + ing), thing (root word + d)	
	. . . .(decide + sion) =	deci<u>sion</u>
	state of being (root word + ed). . . . . (omit + sion) =	omi<u>ssion</u>
some	causes (root word)	trouble<u>some</u>
	group of (root word)	three<u>some</u>
	has a lot of (root word), (a + root word) to a	
	considerable degree	burden<u>some</u>
	inclined to (root word), likely to (root word)	quarrel<u>some</u>
tion	act of (root word + ing), state of (root word + ing)	
	. . . . . (introduce + tion) =	introdu<u>ction</u>
	result of (root word + ing), thing (root word + d)	
	. . . . . .(produce + tion) =	produ<u>ction</u>
	state of being (root word + d) . . . .(reduce + tion) =	redu<u>ction</u>
ty	fact of being (root word), quality of being (root word),	
	state of being (root word).	loyal<u>ty</u>
	(root word) condition.	safe<u>ty</u>
	(root word) tens	six<u>ty</u>
ure	act of (root word + ing)	press<u>ure</u>
	being (root word + d). . . . .(expose + ure) =	expos<u>ure</u>
	result of (root word + ing) . . . .(erase + ure) =	eras<u>ure</u>
	thing that (root word + s) . . . .(legislate + ure) =	legislat<u>ure</u>
	thing that is (root word + ed). . . . .(expose + ure) =	expos<u>ure</u>
ward	in the direction of (root word), toward (root word)	home<u>ward</u>
	toward the (root word + <u>side</u>)	back<u>ward</u>
	with the (root word) facing forward, with the (root word)	
	first.	back<u>ward</u>
wards	in the direction of (root word), toward (root word)	home<u>wards</u>
	toward the (root word + <u>side</u>)	back<u>wards</u>
	with the (root word) facing forward, with the (root word)	
	first.	back<u>wards</u>
ways	in the direction of the (root word), toward the (root	
	word)	edge<u>ways</u>
	with the (root word) facing forward, with the (root word)	
	first.	edge<u>ways</u>
wise	in a (root word) way	like<u>wise</u>
	in a (root word + ing) way.	slant<u>wise</u>
	in the direction of the (root word), toward the (root	
	word)	edge<u>wise</u>
	with the (root word) facing forward, with the (root word)	
	first.	edge<u>wise</u>

y   act of (root word + ing), action of (root word + ing)

        . . . . (inquire + y) =   inquiry

contains (root word), made of (root word), marked by

(root word), of (root word) . . . .   sandy

fact of being (root word), quality of being (root word),

state of being (root word) . . . .   honesty

full of (root word) . . . .(juice + y) =   juicy

inclined to (root word), likely to (root word) . . . .   fussy

like (a + root word), resembles (a + root word), suggests

(a + root word) . . . .   bushy

little (root word), (also used to show affection). . . . .   dolly

somewhat (root word) . . . .   scanty

ROOT WORDS THAT CHANGE

Sometimes a word that I know perfectly well is changed before an ending is added to it. The changed word looks different than it did before it was changed. In addition, this changed word now has an ending added to it. So I might have trouble recognizing this word. But if I know how such a word might be changed, I can be on the look-out for root words that have been changed. Now it will be a lot easier for me to recognize words like that.

Here are some important ways that words might be changed when they become root words:

1. Sometimes the final consonant of a word is doubled before the ending is added:

big	→ biggest	grin	→ grinning
chop	→ chopped	hot	→ hotter
cut	→ cutting	pad	→ padded

(This often happens when the word ends with a single consonant that follows a single vowel.)

2. The word ends with a silent e. Usually the final silent e is dropped before adding an ending that starts with a vowel:

care	→ caring	rise	→ rising
change	→ changing	smile	→ smiling
ride	→ riding	trace	→ tracing

3. The word ends with consonant and y (by, cy, dy, etc.). Usually the y is changed to i before an ending is added:

baby	→ babies	happy	→ happier
fly	→ flies	pony	→ ponies
funny	→ funniest	tiny	→ tiniest

(But if the word ends with vowel and y — ay, ey, etc.: Usually the y does not change to i before the ending is added: turkey → turkeys, play → player, boy → boyish.)

4. The word ends with f or fe. Sometimes the f changes to v before the ending is added:

calf	→ calves	leaf	→ leaves
half	→ halves	shelf	→ shelves
knife	→ knives	wife	→ wives

5. The word ends with the t sound. The t (and the silent e, if there is a silent e) might be dropped before the cy ending is added:

accurate	→ accuracy	infant	→ infancy
agent	→ agency	president	→ presidency
decent	→ decency	vacant	→ vacancy

6. The word ends with the d sound or with the t sound. The d or the t (and the silent e, if there is a silent e) might be dropped, or it might be changed to s before the sion ending is added:

comprehend	→ comprehension	convert	→ conversion
decide	→ decision	revert	→ reversion
recede	→ recession	admit	→ admission
proceed	→ procession	permit	→ permission

MORE ABOUT PREFIXES, ROOTS, AND SUFFIXES

Caution: Do I know thoroughly how a prefix, a root, and a suffix work together to make a new word? Do I understand clearly how the meaning of a prefix, a root, and a suffix together determine what the new word means? If I can answer "yes" to those two questions, I should be ready to tackle the information about Latin and Greek roots. But if there is the slightest doubt in my mind, I should not continue with this section. I should restudy the information about prefixes, suffixes, and English language roots, starting on page 140. I should practice a lot working with prefixes, suffixes, and English language roots. I must restudy and repractice until I am confident of my knowledge and my understanding. Then I will feel at ease when I am working with prefixes, suffixes, and English language roots. Then I should be ready to start working with Latin and Greek roots.

Making English Words from Latin Roots

This discussion about Latin roots and the next discussion, which will be about Greek roots, will tell how a lot of English words were made. These two discussions also will tell why those English words mean what they do mean.

Latin is the language that was used a long time ago by the Romans. Those people had a highly developed civilization. Because of that fact, the Romans, in one way or another, had great influence on the people and on the thinking of the people in many other lands, including England. So in one way or another, the language of Rome — Latin — had great influence on the language in many other lands, including England. Thus it was that many Latin words became a part of the English language. A lot of the English words that we see and read every day are really Latin or partly Latin.

Often our English word does not use all of the Latin word. Instead, the Latin ending was dropped, and we use the remaining part of the Latin word — the root of the Latin word. We call it a Latin root.

The same Latin root might appear in many different English words.

A Latin root might be used in different ways in our

English word. For example, I might see a prefix and a Latin root. Or I might see a Latin root and a suffix. Another time I might see a prefix, a Latin root, and a suffix. Possibly I might see that two Latin roots have been put together to make one English word. But regardless of how the Latin root is used, its meaning stays pretty much the same.

Here, then, is something important for me to think about: So many of our English words have a Latin root in them. Many of these Latin roots are used over and over again in a lot of English words. So if I can recognize the most important prefixes and know what they mean; if I can recognize the most important suffixes and know what they mean; and if I can recognize some of the Latin roots and know what they mean — if I can do those things, then I have a very useful clue that will help me to figure out the meaning of many, many English words that I might not immediately recognize or know.

Sometimes that clue will give me the meaning of the English word right away. Other times I might have to use my imagination along with the clue. But in either case, that clue can be very helpful, especially if it is used together with the sentence meaning clues (see "How I Can Build a Bigger Reading Vocabulary", suggestion 3, on page 63).

Let's examine some of our English words that were made from Latin roots. A meaning of the prefix, the Latin root, and the suffix is given in parenthesis under each. Then we have the complete English word. After that, we have a definition of the English word:

PREFIX AND LATIN ROOT

bi (two)	+ sect (cut)	= bisect	cut or divide into two parts
ex (out)	+ tract (draw)	= extract	pull out; draw out
im (in)	+ port (carry)	= import	bring in from a foreign country
in (in)	+ ject (throw)	= inject	force liquid into something

pre   + dict   = predict   tell beforehand
(before)   (say)

pro   + ceed   = proceed   move forward
(forward)   (move)

re   + pel   = repel   drive back
(back)   (drive)

LATIN ROOT AND SUFFIX

dent   + al   = dental   of or for the teeth
(tooth)   (of)

PREFIX, LATIN ROOT, AND SUFFIX

in   + vis   + ible = invisible   cannot be seen
(not)   (see)   (can be)

TWO LATIN ROOTS MAKE THE ENGLISH WORD

manu   + script   = manuscript   book or paper written
(hand)   (write)   by hand or with a
                                      typewriter

Here is a list of some Latin root forms that help to make up many English language words:

ced, cede, ceed, cess	= go; move
dent	= tooth
dict	= say; tell
duc, duce, duct	= to lead
fer	= bring; carry
gress	= go; step; walk
ject	= throw
man, manu	= hand
miss, mit	= send
pel	= drive
port	= carry
rupt	= break; burst

scrib, scribe, script	=	write
sect	=	to cut
spec, spect, spic	=	look; look at
spir, spire	=	breathe
tract	=	draw (pull)
vers, verse, vert	=	turn
vid, vis	=	see
viv	=	live
voc	=	call; speech; voice

Making English Words from Greek Roots

The ancient Greek people gave many ideas and much knowledge to civilization. Those ideas and that knowledge are responsible for a lot of the ideas and knowledge that we have today.

People need words in order to have ideas and knowledge. We need words in order to think about ideas and knowledge. We need words in order to discuss ideas and knowledge with other people either out loud or in writing.

So we have used words from the language of the ancient Greek people to make the words that we have needed. Those Greek words have made it possible for us to express the ideas and knowledge that have come to us from the ancient Greeks. Those Greek words also have made it possible for us to make English words that name so well many ideas and much knowledge that are more recent in origin (for example, phonograph).

Many of the English language words that we use every day were made from Greek words or from Greek roots. Those English words were made from Greek roots in much the same way that English words were made from Latin roots.

These Greek roots are used over and over in many English language words, just as the Latin roots are. So these Greek roots are very helpful word meaning clues, just as the Latin roots are.

Here are some English language words that were made

from Greek roots:

anthropo (man)	+ logy (study of)	= anthropology	the study of the beginning and development of mankind
geo (earth)	+ graphy (describing)	= geography	the study of the earth's surface, climate, and people
peri (around)	+ meter (measure)	= perimeter	the distance (measure) around the outer boundary of a surface or figure
poly (many)	+ gon (angle)	= polygon	a figure that usually has more than four straight sides and angles
hypo (under)	+ derm + ic (skin) (being)	= hypodermic	under the skin; injected under the skin

Here is a list of some Greek root forms that help to make up many English language words:

anthropo	=	man (human being)
bio	=	life
chron, chrono	=	time
cracy	=	government; rule
derm	=	skin
geo	=	earth
gram	=	something drawn; something written
graph	=	draw; write
graphy	=	describing; recording; writing
logy	=	science of; study of
meter	=	measure
micro	=	small
phil, phile, philo	=	love; loving
phon, phone, phono	=	sound; voice
photo	=	light

psych, psycho	=	mind; soul
scope	=	view
sophy	=	clever; skilled; wisdom; wise
tel, tele	=	distant; far
therm, thermo	=	heat

WHAT IS A SYLLABLE?

A syllable might be a vowel all by itself: a. Or a syllable might be a group of letters that has one vowel sound somewhere in the group: af, plen, fi.

A syllable might be a little word all by itself: sing. Or a syllable might be part of a longer word: af-ter.

The important thing is this: A syllable must have exactly one vowel sound. A syllable cannot have more than one vowel sound, and a syllable cannot have less than one vowel sound. A syllable might have more than one vowel, but only one of those vowels will have a sound. The other vowel or vowels in the syllable will be silent: please. (A vowel sound team or a vowel-consonant team has only one vowel sound: out, na-tion.)

So if I see that a word has one vowel sound, I know that the word has one syllable. If I see that the word has two vowel sounds, I know that the word has two syllables, etc.

Let's see how many syllables these words have:

can . . . . I see 1 vowel sound, so the word has 1 syllable.

cake. . . . . I see 1 vowel sound, so the word has 1 syllable.

boat. . . . . I see 1 vowel sound, so the word has 1 syllable.

please . . . . I see 1 vowel sound, so the word has 1 syllable.

pupil . . . . I see 2 vowel sounds, so the word has 2 syllables.

season . . . . I see 2 vowel sounds, so the word has 2 syllables.

notice. . . . . I see 2 vowel sounds, so the word has 2 syllables.

dusty . . . . I see 2 vowel sounds, so the word has 2 syllables.

remember. . . . . . I see 3 vowel sounds, so the word has 3 syllables.

substitute . . . . . . I see 3 vowel sounds, so the word has 3 syllables.

locomotive . . . . . I see 4 vowel sounds, so the word has 4 syllables.

accommodate. . . . I see 4 vowel sounds, so the word has 4 syllables.

tuberculosis . . . . I see 5 vowel sounds, so the word has 5 syllables.

Reminder to teachers: Remember that the ending ed is not always sounded as a separate syllable. If the root word ends with d or with t, ed is sounded as a separate syllable: needed, waited. Otherwise, ed is not sounded as a separate syllable: asked, rained. In the latter case, the ed sometimes sounds like t to some people (wished). That might happen if ed follows a voiceless consonant sound (such as f, k, p, and sh). Many people, however, claim that they do not hear the t sound at all. Instead, they hear (or they think they hear) the d sound, regardless of whether ed follows a voiced or a voiceless consonant sound.

HOW CAN I DIVIDE A WORD INTO SYLLABLES?

Here is a word that I don't recognize. I see that it has more than one vowel sound, so I know that the word has more than one syllable. How do I split up the word into syllables so that I can sound out the word syllable by syllable?

Well, before I actually divide the word into syllables, there are three things that I should do:

1. I should see whether or not the word is a compound word. If the word is a compound word, and if I look at it carefully, I probably will recognize at least one of the words that makes up the compound word. Suppose that I recognize one of the words, but I don't recognize the other word. In that case, I should now divide the compound word into its different words. I can do that with my finger or with a piece of paper, or I can write the parts on a piece of paper. With the compound word split apart, I might recognize what the other word is.

If I now know what the separate words are, I don't have to divide anything into syllables, because now I will know what the whole compound word is.

If I still don't recognize one of the words, I should try to sound it out. If it has more than one syllable, I now will have to divide the word into syllables and then sound it out. Then I will know what the whole compound word is.

2. I should see whether or not the word has a prefix. If there is a prefix, I should cover it up with my finger or with a piece of paper.

With the prefix out of the way, I might recognize the root word, and I won't have to divide the word into syllables.

3. I should see whether or not the word has a suffix. If there is a suffix, I should cover it up with my finger or with a piece of paper.

With the suffix out of the way, I might recognize the root word, and I won't have to divide the word into syllables.

I have done those three things, and I still have a word on my hands that I don't recognize. What am I supposed to do next?

Well, now I will have to divide the word into syllables. If the word ends with a consonant then le, I will first take care of that part of the word the way we will mention a little later. Then I will return to the beginning of the word. If there is a prefix, I will separate it from the rest of the word. Now I am ready to divide the rest of the word into syllables.

(*Teachers:* We do not have the suffix separated from the root word at this time, because in many cases the last letter of the root word becomes fused with the beginning of the suffix, and sometimes the accent of the root word changes when a suffix is added: ac'-ci-dent ➡ ac'-ci-den'-tal; de-part' ➡ de-par'-ture; in-form' ➡ in'-for-ma'-tion; mu'-sic ➡ mu-si'-cian; se-cure' ➡ se-cu'-ri-ty. More examples of this are on page 176.

(Also, as we have noted in the section, "Root Words that Change", sometimes the last part of a root word is dropped or undergoes a complete change when a suffix is added: ben'-e-fit ➡ ben'-e-fi'-cial — t changes to c, which fuses with the suffix ial to form the cial vowel-consonant team; di-vide' ➡ di-vi'-sion — de is dropped; ex-pand' ➡ ex-pan'-sion — d is dropped.

(For those reasons, we believe it is less confusing and therefore less difficult to a pupil if he handles a suffix as though it were part of the root word when he is trying to divide an unrecognized word into syllables and correctly place the accent.)

This is what I should do to divide the word into syllables:
First, I should count the number of vowel sounds in the word. This will tell me how many syllables I should have when I get through dividing the word into syllables.
Then I should use one of these clues each time I have to divide between syllables:

Clues for Dividing a Word into Syllables

Clue 1.

The Clue: There is a vowel sound, then two consonants to-gether, then another vowel sound: vowel sound, con-sonant, consonant, vowel sound.

What I Do: Usually I will divide the word between the two consonants: vowel sound, consonant ∧ consonant, vowel sound (but not if the consonants form a consonant team: au-thor, ech-o, because a consonant team stays together):

rab-bit	ab-sent	ad-ver-tise
sud-den	shel-ter	en-ter-tain
sup-per	stan-za	pas-sen-ger
blos-som	per-son	wil-der-ness
at-tend	dis-pute	kin-der-gar-ten

Reminder to teachers: Remember that often the vowel sound might be followed by three consonants. When this happens, two of the consonants usually will form a consonant blend or a consonant team and will stay together as though they were a single consonant. So this situation is really like having two consonants together: ad-dress, con-gress, an-chor, far-ther.

Remember also, that the vowel sound might be followed by four consonants. This, again, is simply a variation of having two consonants together, for we might have a combination like one of these: 1) a single consonant and a triple consonant blend: con-script, con-struct; 2) a single consonant and a consonant blend made of a consonant team and a single consonant: an-thra-cite, an-thro-poid; 3) two consonant teams: diph-the-ri-a, diph-thong.

Clue 2A.

The Clue: There is a vowel sound, then only one consonant, then another vowel sound: vowel sound, consonant, vowel sound.

What I Do: Usually I will divide the word just before the single consonant. Then the single consonant will start the next syllable: vowel sound ∧ consonant, vowel sound:

a-corn	sai-lor	co-co-nut

ba-con	tai-lor	po-ta-to
mi-nus	ea-ger	va-ca-tion
clo-ver	rea-son	lo-co-mo-tive
mu-sic	sea-son	se-cu-ri-ty

Clue 2B.

The Clue: The same as for 2A: vowel sound, consonant, vowel sound.

What I Do: I tried to divide the word just before the single consonant, but that didn't work. So I will try to divide the word just after the single consonant: vowel sound, consonant ∧ vowel sound:

cab-in	mag-ic	sec-ond
cam-el	med-al	sev-en
clev-er	nev-er	trav-el
fin-ish	riv-er	vis-it
lem-on	rob-in	wag-on

Clue 3.

The Clue: The word ends with a consonant, then l, then e: consonant le.

What I Do: I will make the consonant le be the last syllable in the word: ∧ consonant le. When I sound out the word, I will make the le sound like el in an unaccented syllable (sort of like ul said very fast and with very little force):

a-ble	jun-gle	en-cir-cle
nee-dle	spar-kle	en-tan-gle
ri-fle	ap-ple	em-bez-zle
ea-gle	whis-tle	per-mis-si-ble
ma-ple	cat-tle	re-li-a-ble

I must be sure to notice that Clue 3 is used only when a word ends with consonant le. And Clue 3 is used only to cut off the consonant le from the rest of the word, so that the consonant le will be the last syllable in the word. This is the only time when Clue 3 can be used.

I must remember, too, that when the word ends with consonant le, I should make the consonant le be the last syllable in the word before I go back to the front of the word and start using Clue 1 or Clue 2. For example, let's take the word embezzle. When I examine the last part of the word to see whether or not it has a suffix, I notice that the word ends with consonant le. So I do this: embez|zle. Now I return to the front of the word. I divide off the prefix, if there is a prefix. Then I start using Clue 1 or Clue 2 on the rest of the word.

Of course, if the word is only a two-syllable word (like rifle), this will be true: After I use Clue 3 (ri|fle), I don't have to use Clue 1 or Clue 2 at all. Because the word can't be divided any more.

ACCENTED SYLLABLES AND
UNACCENTED SYLLABLES

What do we mean by an accented syllable? What do we mean by an unaccented syllable?

This is what we mean: When I accent a syllable in a word, I say that syllable harder or stronger or more clearly or with more force than I say the other syllable or syllables in the word. That syllable — the one that I say harder, etc. — is the accented syllable in that word.

The other syllable or syllables in that word will be the unaccented syllable or syllables. I say the unaccented syllable or syllables softer, weaker, less clearly, and with less force. I also say the unaccented syllable or syllables much faster than I say the accented syllable. Often I say an unaccented syllable so fast and with so little force that I don't give the vowel a chance to give its real sound.

It is important to accent the right syllable when I say a word that has two or more syllables. Why? Because if I accent the wrong syllable, the word just won't sound the way it should sound.

When I say a word that I recognize, I automatically accent the right syllable. I do this without even thinking about it. I accent the right syllable without even realizing that I am accenting anything. In fact, the matter of accenting a syllable doesn't enter my head. I just say the word, and that's all there is to it.

But when I am figuring out a word that I don't recognize, I have to think about which syllable to accent. And I must accent the right syllable so that I will be able to recognize the word after I sound it out.

Why is there such a thing as an accented syllable, and why is there such a thing as an unaccented syllable? Well, accenting syllables makes the spoken language sound better. Think how horribly monotonous the language would sound if we said every syllable with the same force. Accenting syllables also makes it easier to talk. Think how hard it would be to talk if we had to say every syllable with the same force.

The accent mark looks like this: ′. It is used when a person wants to show somebody else which syllable is accented. The accent mark is put just after the accented syllable and just a little bit higher than the letters in the syllable: pen⁄-cil, pa-rade⁄, re-mem⁄-ber. The accent mark is sort of like an arrow pointing down to the syllable that is accented.

A word with four or more syllables might have two accented syllables. (Some very long words might have three accented syllables.) One syllable will be the really strong accented syllable. The other accented syllable (or syllables) will be accented a little bit. Many dictionaries show the stronger accented syllable with a regular accent mark (⁄), which is called the <u>primary</u> accent. These dictionaries usually use one skinny accent <u>mark</u> (′), which is called the <u>secondary</u> accent, to show the syllable that is accented a little bit. So these dictionaries will accent <u>conversation</u> like this: con′-ver-sa⁄-tion.

Sometimes the meaning of a word changes when I accent a different syllable. Here are some examples of that:

1. content:

con⁄-tent   This is a noun. It might mean <u>what is inside</u> something.

con-tent⁄   As a verb, this word might mean <u>to please</u> or <u>to satisfy</u>. As an adjective, this word might mean <u>satisfied</u>. As a noun, this word might mean <u>satisfaction</u>.

2. desert:

des⁄-ert   As a noun, this word might mean <u>a region that has no water or trees</u>. As an adjective, it might mean <u>like a desert</u>.

de-sert⁄   This word is a verb. It might mean <u>to go away and leave</u> somebody.

3. perfect:

per⁄-fect   This word is an adjective. It might mean <u>completely without mistakes</u>.

per-fect⁄   This word is a verb. It might mean <u>to</u>

remove <u>all</u> <u>of</u> <u>the</u> <u>mistakes</u> <u>from</u> something.

4. progress:

prog′-ress   This word is a noun. It might mean <u>improvement</u>.

pro-gress′   This word is a verb. It might mean <u>to</u> <u>get</u> <u>better</u>.

5. project:

proj′-ect   This word is a noun. It might mean <u>something</u> <u>a</u> <u>person</u> <u>is</u> <u>trying</u> <u>to</u> <u>do</u>.

pro-ject′   This word is a verb. It might mean <u>to</u> <u>stick</u> <u>out</u>.

In a note to teachers on page 170, we mentioned that the accent of a word might change when a suffix is added. Here are some more examples of that accent change taking place:

ad′-verb	⟶	ad-ver′-bi-al
ap-ply′	⟶	ap′-pli-ca′-tion
ath′-lete	⟶	ath-let′-ic
at′-om	⟶	a-tom′-ic
civ′-il	⟶	ci-vil′-ian
he′-ro	⟶	he-ro′-ic
hu′-man	⟶	hu-man′-i-ty
mel′-o-dy	⟶	me-lo′-di-ous
meth′-od	⟶	me-thod′-i-cal
nor′-mal	⟶	nor-mal′-i-ty
rap′-id	⟶	ra-pid′-i-ty
sol′-id	⟶	so-lid′-i-fy′

Why does the accent shift like that? Often, the shifting of the accent seems to make the word easier to pronounce. Also, the accent might change because the accent clue has changed. (We will discuss the accent clues a little later.)

I realize that it is important to accent the right syllable in a word. But how do I know what the right syllable is? How do I know which syllable I should accent?

One important thing I can do is to start listening carefully to words. I should practice listening for the accented syllable or syllables of the words. After a while, that should help me to get a better understanding of the whole business of accenting. This is a lot like watching a top-notch basketball player shooting baskets. It gives me good ideas that I couldn't have gotten any other way.

In our language, there are two patterns of accent that show up often. They will be a help to me. Also, there are some clues that many times will tell me correctly which syllable I should accent. These clues work often enough to make it worthwhile for me to learn them. They, too, will be a help to me. In many words, I will be able to use the accent clue information and the accent pattern information together.

Patterns of Accent

Accent Pattern 1:

Every other syllable is accented: The first syllable is accented, the second syllable is not accented, the third syllable is accented, the fourth syllable is not accented, etc.: <u>yes</u>, <u>no</u>, <u>yes</u>, <u>no</u>, etc. **Or** the first syllable is not accented, the second syllable is accented, the third syllable is not accented, etc.: <u>no</u>, <u>yes</u>, <u>no</u>, etc.

con′-ver-sa′-tion	lo′-co-mo′-tive
dis′-ap-pear′-ance	oc′-cu-pa′-tion
in′-de-pen′-dence	pres′-i-den′-tial

OR

com-pan′-ion	ap-pre′-ci-a′-tion
e-lec′-tric	de-nom′-i-na′-tor
sub-trac′-tion	tu-ber′-cu-lo′-sis

178

Accent Pattern 2:

There is an accented syllable and then two unaccented syllables: <u>yes</u>, <u>no</u>, <u>no</u>.

con′-so-nant   pos′-si-ble

dif′-fer-ent   sin′-gu-lar

pas′-sen-ger   vic′-to-ry

Some words contain both accent patterns: re-spon′-si-bil′-i-ty (<u>no</u>, <u>yes</u>, <u>no</u>, <u>yes</u>, no, no), com′-pre-hen′-si-bil′-i-ty (<u>yes</u>, <u>no</u>, <u>yes</u>, <u>no</u>, <u>yes</u>, <u>no</u>, <u>no</u>).

Minor Accent Patterns:

Here is an accent pattern that happens sometimes but does not happen often: pay′-day′, pay′-mas′-ter, e-lec′-tric′-i-ty (a pattern in which two syllables next to each other are both accented).

Here is another accent pattern that happens sometimes but does not happen often: de-ter′-mi-na-ble (a pattern in which three unaccented syllables are together).

Clues for Accenting Syllables

Clue 1.

The Clue: The word ends with <u>ic</u>.

What I Do: Usually I will accent the syllable just before <u>ic</u>:

arc′-<u>tic</u>   ar-tis′-<u>tic</u>

com′-<u>ic</u>   ath-let′-<u>ic</u>

mu′-<u>sic</u>   gi-gan′-<u>tic</u>

If the word has four or more syllables, I probably will also have to accent another syllable at or near the beginning of the word. (Notice how the accent patterns are working):

ac′-ro-bat′-<u>ic</u>   a-pol′-o-get′-<u>ic</u>

an'-ti-sep'-t<u>ic</u>   di'-a-gram-mat'-<u>ic</u>

sym'-pa-thet'-<u>ic</u>   en-thu'-si-as'-t<u>ic</u>

Clue 2.

The Clue: The word ends with one of these vowel-conso-
nant teams: <u>cial</u>, <u>cian</u>, <u>cient</u>, <u>cious</u>, <u>ion</u>, <u>sion</u>, <u>sive</u>,
<u>tial</u>, <u>tion</u>, <u>tious</u>, <u>ture</u>, and often <u>tive</u>. (This clue works
better with the other teams than it does with <u>tive</u>).

What I Do: Usually I will <u>not</u> accent one of those teams.
Usually I <u>will</u> accent the syllable just before one of
those teams:

com-mer'-<u>cial</u>   pro-gres'-<u>sive</u>

mu-si'-<u>cian</u>   es-sen'-<u>tial</u>

suf-fi'-<u>cient</u>   sub-trac'-<u>tion</u>

de-li'-<u>cious</u>   in-fec'-<u>tious</u>

o-pin'-<u>ion</u>   de-par'-<u>ture</u>

con-clu'-<u>sion</u>   at-ten'-<u>tive</u>

If the word has four or more syllables, I probably
will also have to accent another syllable at or near the
beginning of the word:

ar'-ti-fi'-<u>cial</u>   ap'-pre-hen'-<u>sive</u>

pol'-i-ti'-<u>cian</u>   con'-fi-den'-<u>tial</u>

co'-ef-fi'-<u>cient</u>   in'-for-ma'-<u>tion</u>

av'-a-ri'-<u>cious</u>   con'-sci-en'-<u>tious</u>

mul'-ti-mil'-<u>lion</u>   man'-u-fac'-<u>ture</u>

com'-pre-hen'-<u>sion</u>   lo'-co-mo'-<u>tive</u>

au'-thor-i-za'-<u>tion</u>   de-ter'-mi-na'-<u>tion</u>

con-sol'-i-da'-<u>tion</u>   i-mag'-i-na'-<u>tion</u>

180

Clue 3.

The Clue: An i̲ is by itself in a syllable.

or

An i̲ is at the end of a syllable.

What I Do: Usually I will accent the syllable just before i̲:

cit/-i̲-zen	com-par/-i̲-son
dec/-i̲-mal	di-gest/-i̲-ble
par/-ti̲-cle	a-lu/-mi̲-num
u/-ni̲-form	ma-te/-ri̲-al

If the word has five or more syllables, I probably will also have to accent another syllable in the word:

de-nom/-i̲-na/-tor	u/-ni̲-ver/-si̲-ty
au-thor/-i̲-tar/-i̲-an	am-bas/-sa-do/-ri̲-al

Sometimes in a three syllable word or a four syllable word, it might be necessary to accent another syllable, too:

ded/-i̲-cate/	an-tic/-i̲-pate/
at/-ti̲-tude/	com-mu/-ni̲-cate/

Caution: Clue 3 usually will not work if the i̲ is just before a vowel-consonant team listed in Clue 2. Clue 2 is a stronger clue than Clue 3:

am-bi̲/-tion	ben/-e-fi̲/-cial
de-li̲/-cious	su/-per-sti̲/-tious
a-rith/-me-ti̲/-cian	math/-e-ma-ti̲/-cian

Clue 4.

The Clue: The word ends with consonant and le (ble, cle, dle, etc.)

What I Do: Usually I will <u>not</u> accent that syllable:

      can′-<u>dle</u>   en-cir′-<u>cle</u>

      ma′-<u>ple</u>   ex-am′-<u>ple</u>

      whis′-<u>tle</u>   mir′-a-<u>cle</u>

      de-pend′-a-<u>ble</u>   kil′-o-cy′-<u>cle</u>

      di-gest′-i-<u>ble</u>

Clue 5.

The Clue: The word ends with a suffix.

What I Do: Usually I will <u>not</u> accent the suffix:

      draw′-<u>ing</u>   a-gree′-<u>ment</u>

      hope′-<u>ful</u>   em-ploy′-<u>er</u>

      soft′-<u>ness</u>   re′-cent-<u>ly</u>

      his-to′-ri-<u>an</u>   va-ca′-tion-<u>ist</u>

      pres′-i-den-<u>cy</u>

Clue 6.

The Clue: The word ends with <u>consonant</u> and <u>y</u> (<u>by</u>, <u>cy</u>, <u>dy</u>, etc.) The word has two or three syllables.

What I Do: Usually I will accent the first syllable:

      am′-p<u>ly</u>   sen′-si-b<u>ly</u>

      can′-<u>dy</u>   va′-can-<u>cy</u>

      dai′-<u>sy</u>   vic′-to-<u>ry</u>

If this doesn't work, often it's because the word is a verb. A verb that ends with <u>consonant</u> and <u>y</u> usually uses a different accent pattern. So this is what I should do:

If the word has two syllables: I should accent the second syllable instead of the first syllable.

If the word has three syllables: Usually I should

use a strong accent for the first syllable and a weak accent for the last syllable:

de-<u>ny</u>′   mul′-ti-p<u>ly</u>′

re-pl<u>y</u>′   sim′-pli-<u>fy</u>′

sup-pl<u>y</u>′   oc′-cu-<u>py</u>′

Clue 7.

The Clue: The word ends with <u>consonant</u> and <u>y</u>. The word has four or more syllables.

What I Do: Usually I will <u>not</u> accent the syllable that has the <u>consonant</u> and <u>y</u>:

a-cad′-e-<u>my</u>   ad-mon′-i-to′-<u>ry</u>

ca-pac′-i-<u>ty</u>   an′-thro-pol′-o-<u>gy</u>

ter′-ri-to′-<u>ry</u>   ap′-pen-dec′-to-<u>my</u>

Once in a while the word will be a verb. If the word is a verb, usually I will use a strong accent for the second syllable and a weak accent for the last syllable:

i-den′-ti-<u>fy</u>′   so-lid′-i-<u>fy</u>′

Clue 8.

The Clue: The word ends with one of these vowel-consonant teams: <u>age</u>, <u>ous</u>.

What I Do: Usually I will <u>not</u> accent one of these teams.

If the word has two syllables: Usually I will accent the syllable before the team (the first syllable):

pack′-<u>age</u>   fa′-m<u>ous</u>

If the word has three or four syllables: Usually I will leave one unaccented syllable between the team and the accented syllable:

av′-er-<u>age</u>   ad-ven′-tur-<u>ous</u>

If the word has five or more syllables: I probably will also have to accent another syllable at or near the beginning of the word:

cer′-e-mo′-ni-ous   con-tem′-po-ra′-ne-ous

Note to teachers: As you know, many textbooks and workbooks say that a prefix usually is not accented. Although it is true that a prefix often is unaccented, we have not included that as a clue in this book, because our search of dictionaries revealed too many cases in which a prefix is accented. Therefore, we felt that using a prefix situation as a clue would confuse a pupil rather than help him.

Note about accent marks: In "Accented Syllables and Unaccented Syllables", we have used real, printed accent marks — the kind of accent marks that printed books (such as textbooks and dictionaries) usually use. These printed accent marks slant toward the accented syllable: ╱ and ╲.

Teachers and other people might make accent marks with a typewriter. Accent marks made by a typewriter will be shaped a lot like printed accent marks, but the typewriter-made accent marks will not slant toward the accented syllable. Instead, the accent marks made by a typewriter point straight down right after the accented syllable: ' and '. We have used this kind of accent marks in other places in Johnny's Reading Skills.

When teachers or other people make accent marks by hand, the accent marks probably will slant toward the accented syllable, and might be shaped something like printed accent marks if the person can draw fairly well or if he has a lot of time and patience. Often, though, the handmade accent marks will look more like short lines slanting toward the accented syllable: ╱ and ╲.

SECTION 18

WHAT I CAN DO TO FIGURE OUT
A WORD THAT I DON'T RECOGNIZE

There is no one best way to figure out words. There is no one best method that I can use for all words. One method might work very well for some words, but that method might not work at all well for other words.

So I should know several ways to go about figuring out words that I don't recognize. Then if the first method I try doesn't work, I will be able to try some other method. I might have to use more than one method for some words.

I want to use the method that will help me to figure out the word correctly as fast as possible.

Here are some of the things that I can do and some of the things that I should not do:

1. I should not just guess. I should not say the first thing that pops into my mind without thinking.

2. I should use good, clear thinking.

3. If there is a picture or some other kind of illustration on the page, I should see if there is some clue in the illustration that will help me to figure out what the word is.

4. I should notice the beginning sound of the word, and I should look on through the rest of the word. I should finish reading the sentence. Then I should ask myself, "What must this word be in order to make sense in the sentence and also have the sounds that I noticed?"

5. Does part of the word look like part of a word that I already know? If a part of one word looks like a part of another word, there is a very good chance that the part will sound alike in both words, too. (This is not always true, but it usually is true.)

For example, let's take the words night and slight. Of course, I know both words. But just suppose that I do know night but that I don't recognize slight. So I say to myself, "Well, the ight probably sounds the same in both words.

So all I have to do is think of how <u>night</u> sounds, then change the n to <u>sl</u> and say the word. And I will have the new word <u>slight</u>."

6. It also will help me to notice the shape and the length of the word.

For example, if I see a long word, I know that I will have to sound or say a long word. But if I see just a short word, I will have to sound or say a short word.

Reminder to teachers: This sounds so obvious. Often, however, it is not as obvious as it would seem to be. Many times a student without thinking will say a word that is all out of proportion to the size of the word that he or she sees.

7. When I sound out a word, I should be on the lookout for groups of letters that have a sound that I know. (I am talking about such things as consonant teams, vowel sound teams, and vowel-consonant teams.)

8. When I sound out a word, I should remember that some letters have more than one sound. If one sound does not work for a letter like that, I should try another sound for that letter. (I am talking about letters like <u>c</u>, <u>g</u>, <u>s</u>, all of the vowels, some of the vowel sound teams, and some of the vowel-consonant teams.)

9. When I sound out a word, I should remember that some letters might be silent.

10. When I sound out a syllable (or a one-syllable word), I should not stop or pause between the sound of one letter and the sound of the next letter. First I should think the sound of the letters that I see together in the syllable, then I should say the syllable.

I should not think or say a sound like "uh" between the sound of one letter and the sound of the next letter. And I should not make such a sound between syllables when I sound out a word with more than one syllable.

Once I start sounding out a syllable, the sound of one letter should join the sound of the next letter smoothly and without a break in sound.

11. If the word has more than one syllable, I might have to divide the word into syllables before I can sound it out. (See "How Can I Divide a Word into Syllables?" on pages 169-173.)

12. I have tried the methods that have been described, but I still can't figure out the word. What can I do now?

I can look up the word in a dictionary. When I find the word, I will look just after the word. Here is the same word in parenthesis, but here the word is not spelled the way it normally looks. In parenthesis, the word is spelled the way it sounds. That plus the key words at the bottom of the dictionary page will help me to sound out the word.

13. If the word is in a sentence, I should always be sure that the word I figure out makes sense in the sentence.

If the word doesn't make sense in the sentence, I must have made a mistake. Then I will have to try to figure out the word again.

14. I have figured out the word correctly. Is there any-thing else for me to do about the word?

There certainly is something else for me to do. It is very important, too.

I should notice things about the word that will help me to remember the word. The things that I notice should help me to remember what the word looks like and what the word sounds like. Then the next time I see that word, I will recognize it right away. I will not have to take the time to figure out that word all over again.

Some of those suggestions might sound awfully long and drawn-out. Actually they are not long and drawn-out if I know them thoroughly and have had plenty of practice using them.

INDEX

Accelerators, reading: using 74

Accent: primary 175, 181-182, 183; secondary 175, 181-182, 183

Accent changes: meaning of some words affected by 175-176; reasons for 176-177; suffix causing 170, 176-177

Accent clues: accent pattern used with 177, 178-179; change in 176-177; described 178-183

Accent marks: discussed 174-175, 183

Accent patterns: accent clues used with 177, 178-179; described 177-178; verb ending with *consonant* and *y* 181-182

Accented syllables: *see* Syllables, accented

Accenting syllables: *see* Syllables, accenting

Active mind: needed when reading 17-18, 26, 29, 53

Alert mind: *see* Active mind

Alphabet: list of 93

Answers for questions: finding 80-84; thinking while looking for 80, 81, 82-83, 83. *See also* Tests, taking

Anxious, being: before tests 35; need to stop 11

Attention: need for, while reading 52

Author's meanings: ability to interpret 59

Base words: *see* Roots

Because-type answers on tests 42

Bird's-eye view of lessons 24

Books. finding answers for questions in 80-84; finding information for reports in 86-89; skimming 52-53, 75, 78-79, 87, 88

Brakes on reading speed 73

Calmness: before tests 35; during tests 39, 40

Captions: help find answers 81, 83; used when studying 25

Carry-over of learning: *see* Transfer of learning

Catchy word trick: remembering information helped by using 37

Causes: *how* test questions asking for 43; *why* test questions asking for 42

Central thought: *see* Ideas, main

Character identification: in fiction-type reading 56, 59

Charts: *see* Illustrations

Clue words: use of, helps skimming for answers 80-81, 81, 82-83, 83

Compound words: discussed 139; examples of 139; syllable division and 169

Comprehension: active and alert mind helps 17-18, 26, 29, 53; curiosity and interest help 26; getting ready for reading helps 17, 19, 22, 24-26, 28, 28-29, 52-53, 78-79, 80; grouping words to help 13-14, 53; improving 48-60; lesson organization knowledge helps 19-23, 24-25, 28-29, 78-79; meaning of 48; punctuation marks affect 48-49, 58, 63; questioning helps 17, 24, 26, 27, 28, 29, 29-30, 52-53, 55-56, 78; reading speed and 66-71, 72, 73; skim-previewing helps 17, 19, 24-25, 28, 28-29, 52-53, 78-79; study skills knowledge helps 16, 16-17, 17-18; suggestions for improving 48-57, referred to 27, 29, 36; teachers need to stress suggestions 57; thinking helps 17, 17-18, 27, 53, 80; word-by-word reading affects 14, 53; word meaning knowledge affects 48, 58, 61, 62-63, 63-64, 67; word recognition ability affects 48, 63-64. *See also* Paragraphs; Understanding

Comprehension skills: list of 57-60. *See also* Comprehension

Concentration: during tests 39; when reading 52; when studying for tests 33

Conclusions: forming valid 60

Confidence: before tests 35; during tests 39; getting, in using vowels 107

Conjunctions: discussed 50-52; examples of 50-52

Connecting (relating) mentally: new ideas with familiar 54-55,60; new information with familiar 36, 54-55, 60

Connectives: *see* Conjunctions

Consonant blends: discussed 100, 104, 171; examples of 100-101

Consonant l e, words ending with: accenting 180-181; sound of *le* in 172; syllable division of 169-170, 172-173

Consonant sounds: *see* Consonants

Consonant teams: discussed 102-103, 104, 171; listed and described 102-103; using, to figure out unrecognized words 185

Consonant *y:* explained 98-99; listed 93, 95; sound borrowed by *i* 133, 136-137

Consonants: double 105; doubling final consonant 159; list of 93; silent 104-105, 128, 135, 136, 137, 185; single 95-99; sounds of 95-105; with different sounds 96-99, 185. *See also* Consonant blends; Consonant teams; Freaks

Context clues: *see* Word meaning; Word recognition

Critical reading and thinking 60

Curiosity and interest: developing 25, 26, 28, 29, 78; importance of 26, 29; remembering information helped by 36

Daily assignments: getting ready for tests with 33; tricks used when studying 37

Day of test 34-35

Derivatives: *ur* in 123

Details: reading speed and 70; skimming for 75. *See also* Facts; Information; Paragraphs

Devices, mechanical: using 74

Diagrams: *see* Illustrations; Lessons

Dictionaries: accent marks shown in 175, 183; accenting prefixes 183; double consonants 105; key words in 186; using 17, 62-63, 65, 135, 186; words in parenthesis in 186

Easy reading materials: *see* Reading materials

Eating: affects test preparation 33

Endings: *see* Suffixes

English roots: *see* Roots

Essay tests: *see* Tests, taking

Evaluating: facts and opinions 60; points of view 60

Exaggeration: example of 58

Examples: when to give, on tests 41

Exceptions to vowel sound clues: *see* Vowel sound clues

Exercise, physical: affects test preparation 33

Facts: critical reading and thinking 60; hard-to-remember 33-34, 34, 36-38; paragraph patterns and 17-18; reading speed and 69-70, 70; remembering 34, 36-38, 58, 69, 70; skimming for 75; test review 33. *See also* Details; Information; Paragraphs

Faith: needed for success 11

Familiarity with subject: affects reading speed 68, 70

Fiction-type reading: identifying with character in 56, 59; mental pictures formed while reading 53-54, 58; reading speed and 69-70, 70, 73; sensory imagery in 53-54, 58; skimming and 52, 53, 75; suggestions for improving 52-55, 56-57. *See also* Magazines

Figurative language: examples of 58

Figuring out words: *see* Word recognition

Films, reading: using 74

Finding information: for reports 85-89; for term papers 85-89; in books 86-89; in lessons 29; in magazines 89; reading speed and 69, 70; skimming helps 75, 80-83, 85, 86-89; to answer questions 80-84, thinking while 80, 81, 82-83, 83

Fish hook, baited: using old knowledge like 55

Flexible reader: developing ability to be 66-71

Forgetting: recovery from, by retelling review 28, 30; reducing 27, 28, 29-30, 33-34, 34, 55-56, 56-57; wastes time 28. *See also* Remembering

Formula trick: remembering information helped by using 37

Freaks: list of some 135-137; meaning of 108, 133, 135; type of exception to vowel sound clues 108

French language: some letter sounds from 102, 137

Gadgets: using 74

General ideas: *see* Ideas, general

Generalizations: forming valid 60

Get Ready To Read: part of study system 25-26, 28, 29

Graphs: *see* Illustrations

Greek: contribution to civilization 164; contribution to English language 164; roots in English words

161, 164-166
Grouping words: to get sentence meaning 13-14, 53
Guessing: when figuring out unrecognized words 184

Habits: development of 12, 15-16, 30, 75-76; forming, from suggestions 12; reading speed and 71-73. *See also* Practice, regular; Skill development
Hard reading materials: *see* Reading materials
Hard-to-remember information: learning 33-34, 34, 36-38
Hard work: needed for success 11
Head movements: affect reading speed 73
Health: affects test preparation 33
Help: asking for 56-57, 65
Hobbies: making time for 72

I: borrowing consonant *y* sound 133, 136-137
Ideas: fixing in mind 28, 29, 30, 55-56; forgetting of, reduced 28, 30, 55-56; fuzzy 30; general (overall) picture of 26, 29; Greek people gave 164; hazy 30, 56; looking for 26, 29, 53; mentally connecting (relating) new with familiar 54-55, 60; organizing 16-17, 28, 30, 32, 53, 55-56, during test preparation 32, during tests 32, 39-40, 40; reading speed affected by 67; related 21, 24-25, 27, 28, 29, 53, 55, 62, 78; relating (connecting) 24-25, 27, 28, 29, 53, 55, 62, 78; relationship of, with whole lesson 24-25, 28-29; remembering 16-17, 19, 24-25, 26, 27, 28, 29, 29-30, 32, 53, 55-56; rough 75; understanding 24-25, 26, 29, 29-30, 32, 53, 55-56, 62; unrelated 24; words needed for 164. *See also* Ideas, general; Ideas, important; Ideas, main; Information; Reviewing; Self-quizzes; Skimming; Study-type reading
Ideas, general: meaning of 69, 70; of what information is like 81-82, 83, 87, 88-89; of what lesson is about 24, 25, 28, 52, 78; of what section of lesson is about 26, 29; reading speed affected by reading for 69-70, 70. *See also* Ideas;

Ideas, important; Ideas, main
Ideas, important: fixing in mind 30; forgetting of, reduced 28, 29-30; knowing 32; learning 19; looking for 29; organizing 30, 32; previewing for 24-25; recognizing 19; remembering 19, 32; skimming for 24-25; strengthening in mind 28, 32; summary of lesson states 23; tests and 32; understanding 32. *See also* Ideas; Ideas, general; Ideas, main; Lessons
Ideas, main: creating 15, 21-22, 24, 27; developing 15, 19-22, 23, 24, 25-26, 27, 58, 78; discussing 78; explaining 15, 25-26, 27, 58; finding 29; preventing waste of time studying 28; proving 15; relationship between 21, 22, 24, 25-26, 27, 28, 28-29, 55, 78; relationship between information and 15, 21-22, 24-25, 27, 28, 28-29, 55, 58, 62. *See also* Ideas; Ideas, general; Ideas, important; Lessons; Paragraphs; Sections of a lesson
Illustrations: clues to word meanings 63; figuring out unrecognized words helped by 184; finding answers for questions helped by 81, 83; used before reading 24, 25, 52, 78; used when preparing for tests 33
Imagination: using, while reading 53-54, 56, 58, 59; using, with Latin roots 162
Implications: meaning of 59
Imply: *see* Implications
Important ideas: *see* Ideas, important
Important things to remember: selecting 15, 60; summary of lesson states 23
In what way: kind of *how* test question 43
Indexes: using 83-84, 87, 88
Infer: *see* Inferences
Inferences: importance of 59, 60; meaning of 59
Information: critical reading and thinking 60; determining importance of 15; finding 29; fixing in mind 28, 29, 30, 36-38, 56, 69; forgetting of, reduced 28, 29-30, 56, 64, during tests 39-40, 43, 44; general idea about 81-82, 83, 87, 88-89; general (overall) picture of 26, 29; looking for 26, 27, 29, 53, 69,

70, 75; mentally connecting (relating) new with familiar 36, 54-55, 60; organizing 16-17, 28, 30, 32, 53, 55-56, 69, 70, during test preparation 32, during tests 32, 39-40, 40; picturing in mind 36, 53-54, 58; recognizing important 19; related 24-25, 53; relating (connecting) 24-25, 28, 29, 62; relationship between main ideas and 15, 21-22, 24-25, 27, 28, 28-29, 55, 58, 62; remembering 15, 16, 16-17, 19, 24-25, 26, 27, 28, 29, 29-30, 32, 33-34, 36-38, 43, 53, 56, 58, 60, 69, 70; selecting, to remember 15, 60; strengthening in mind 28, 29-30; summary of lesson states 23; Test Reminders Paper 33-34, 34; tests and 32, 39, 40-43; thinking about 36, 53, 69; tricks help to remember 37-38; understanding 24-25, 26, 29, 29-30, 32, 36, 53, 55-56, 62, 69, 70, 107, 108; unrelated 24. *See also* Details; Facts; Ideas; Lessons; Paragraphs; Reviewing; Self-quizzes; Skimming; Study-type reading

Interest and curiosity: *see* Curiosity and interest

Interpret: meaning of 59

Introduction to lessons 22

Jingle trick: remembering information helped by using 37

Jittery, getting: during tests 40

Key words: in dictionaries 186; in reading material 58

Knowledge: Greek people gave 164; study skills 16, 16-17, 17-18; test preparation strengthens 32; using old to get new 54-55; words needed for 164

Latin: influence on other languages 161; roots in English words 161-164, 164

Learning: curiosity and interest affect 25, 26, 28, 29; listening helps 61-62, 177; quizzing self (reciting) helps 17, 18, 27, 28, 29-30, 55-56; reading speed and 66-71, 73; Review Words Notebook helps 65; test preparation affects 32; transfer of, from reading class to other classes 57; tricks to help 37-38. *See also* Practice, regular; Questioning; Reading carefully; Reviewing; Self-quizzes; Study-type reading

Lessons: bird's-eye view of 24; diagram of 22; general information about 22; general (overall) picture of 24-25, 28-29, 52, 78; important ideas in 19, 25; introduction to 22; main idea of 21, 22, 24, 62, 78; main ideas of 19-22, 23, 24-25, 25-26, 27, 28, 28-29, 29-30, 55-56, 62, 78-79, 80; meaning of, in this book 19; organization of 19-23, 24, 24-25, 28-29, 78; outline of 19-22, 23, 78, used during test preparation 34; pattern or plan of 19-23, 24, 24-25, 78, found by skimming 24, 24-25, 78; skim-previewing 17, 19, 24-25, 28, 28-29, 52-53, 78-79, 80; studying 16, 16-17, 17-18, 19-30, 52-56, 56-57, 69, 70, 72, 75, 75-76, 78-79, 80, using illustrations 24, 25, 52, 78; summary of 23; title of 19, 21, 22, 24, 52, 78; understanding 16, 62-63, 79. *See also* Ideas, general; Ideas, main; Reading carefully; Reading faster; Sections of a lesson; Study-type reading; Subtitles

Letters: *see* Consonants; Vowels

Letters, groups of: using, to help figure out unrecognized words 185

Letters, sounds of: knowledge of, helps figure out unrecognized words 185. *See also* Consonants; Vowels

Library: getting books for reports 86-87, 88; getting magazines for reports 89

Life-like reading 53-54

Lip movements: breaking habit 72-73; reading speed affected by 72

Listening: helps build vocabulary 61-62; helps understand accenting 177

Long vowel sounds: *see* Vowel sounds, long

Looking at words: is not reading 48, 53; reading speed affected by 72

Looking back when reading: affects reading speed 72

Machines, reading: using 74

Magazines: finding information in, for reports 89; skimming 75, 89

Main ideas: *see* Ideas, main

Maps: *see* Illustrations

Mechanical devices: using 74

Memory: fixing hard-to-remember information in 33-34, 34, 36-38; on tests 40; strengthening, while studying 28, 29-30, 32, 55-56, 57, 69, words 65, 135, 186; tricks help 37-38
Mental alertness: see Active mind
Mental health: affects test preparation 33
Mental warm-up: before starting to read 52-53, 78
Mentally connecting: see Connecting (relating) mentally
Metaphors: example of 58
Minds: training 56-57
Mouth: using, while reading silently 72

Nervous, getting: during tests 40
New words: see Vocabulary; Word meaning; Word recognition; Words
Newspapers: skimming 75
Night before tests 33, 34
Notebooks: for review words 65
Notes: taking 60, 82, 83, 87-88, 89; test preparation using class 34, using study 34; Test Reminders Paper 33-34, 34, 36

Objective tests: see Tests, taking
Opinions: in critical reading and thinking 60; part of paragraph patterns 18
Oral reading: affects reading speed 73

Paragraphs: details in 15, 58; facts in 15, 58; information in 15, 19-21, 21-22, 26, 27, 29, 55; main idea of 15-18, 19-21, 21-22, 26, 27, 29-30, 55-56, 58, 62; meaning of, depending on word meaning 62; patterns of 16-18, 58; study of 15-18, 19-21, 21-22, 26-27, 29-30, 55-56; topic sentence of 15, 16. See also Study-type reading; Subtitles
Parts of body: needed for silent reading 73
Parts of speech: changed by accent 175-176; changed by suffixes 149-150; listed 149
Patience: needed for success 11
Patterns of accent: see Accent patterns
Perception, visual: reading speed influenced by see Seeing and thinking; tachistascope quickens 74

Personification: example of 58
Physical health: affects test preparation 33
Picture clues: using, to help figure out unrecognized words 184
Pictures: see Illustrations
Picturing information in mind: remembering information helped by 36; while reading 53-54, 58
Pleasure reading: see Fiction-type reading
Pointing at words: affects reading speed 73
Points of view: in critical reading and thinking 60
Practice, regular: habits developed by 12, 15-16, 30; prefix, suffix, and English root understanding needs 161; reading speed habits changed by 71-73; skimming developed by 75-76; vowel sound understanding needs 107; word attack skills developed by 186. See also Skill development; Suggestions; Using in-information
Prefixes: accenting 183; caution about using examples of 141-142; examples of 140-149; Greek roots with 164-165; importance of 140; introduction to examples of 141-142; Latin roots with 161-163; list of many 141-149; meaning of 140; syllable division and 169, 170, 173; understanding of, needed 161. See also Roots; Word meaning; Word recognition
Previewing: before reading 17, 19, 22, 24-25, 28, 28-29, 52-53, 75, 78-79, 80
Primary accent: see Accent
Pronouns: see Substitute words
Punctuation marks: importance of 48-49, 58, 63
Purpose for reading: affects reading speed 68-70, 70

Question: see Questioning
Questioning: after reading 17, 18, 27, 28, 29-30, 55-56; before reading 17, 24, 25-26, 28, 29, 52-53, 78; how much to read before self- 29, 56; importance of 26, 29, 52-53, 55-56; words for, on tests 40-43; words to use when 25-26, 29, 52, 55. See also Questions
Questions: after reading 55; before

reading 24, 25-26, 29, 52-53, 80; finding answers for 80-84, thinking while 80, 81,82-83, 83; looking for answers to, while reading 26, 53; paragraph patterns include 16, 17; paragraph's main idea found with 15; test 34, 39-47. *See also* Questioning

Quizzes: *see* Self-quizzes; Tests, getting ready for; Tests, taking

Quotation marks: using 82, 83, 87-88, 89

Rapid reading: *see* Reading faster

Rate of reading: *see* Reading speed

Reaction time: quickening *see* Tachistascopes

Read: *see* Reading; Reading carefully; Reading faster; Study-type reading

Readers' Guide to Periodical Literature: using 89

Reading: ability importance mentioned 43; active and alert mind needed while 17-18, 26, 29, 53; amount of, before self-quiz (reciting) 29, 56; between the lines 59; coming alive in mind 53-54; critical 60; dictionary used when 17, 62-63; getting ready for 17, 19, 22, 24-26, 28, 28-29, 52-53, 78-79, 80; grouping words during 13-14, 53; important thing when 62, 66; improving 48-60; looking while 26, 27, 53, 54, 69, 70; meaning of 48, 53; parts of body needed for silent 73; stopping, to think 69; thinking while 17, 17-18, 27, 53, 80; timed 73; understanding 48, 49, 49-52, 55-56,59-60, 61, 62-63, 66, 67, 69, 70, 73, 74; vocabulary-building helped by 64. *See also* Comprehension; Facts; Fiction-type reading; Ideas; Ideas, general; Ideas, important; Ideas, main; Information; Reading carefully; Reading faster; Study-type reading; Word-by-word reading

Reading carefully: concentration 52; fiction 56; hard-to-remember information 36; information for answering questions 82, 83; information for reports 87-88, 89; lessons 16, 16-17, 17-18, 19, 24-25, 26, 26-27, 28, 29-30, 52-56, 56-57, 69, 70, 72, 80; reading faster or reading

slower 66-71; test directions 39; test questions 39, 44-45. *See also* Comprehension; Study-type reading; Understanding

Reading comprehension: *see* Comprehension

Reading critically 60

Reading faster: concentration 52; information for answering questions 81-82, 83; information for reports 87, 88-89; lessons 26, 29; reading slower or 66-71; suggestions for 71-74. *See also* Reading speed

Reading flexibility: developing 66-71

Reading for pleasure: *see* Fiction-type reading

Reading materials: affect reading speed 66-68, 70, 73

Reading purpose: affects reading speed 68-70, 70

Reading rate: *see* Reading speed

Reading situations: affect reading speed 66-67, 70

Reading speed: comprehension and 66-71, 72, 73; depends on individual 71; flexibility development 66-71; how fast a person can read 73; how fast a person should read 74; importance of increasing 72; increasing 71-74; most important thing to remember about 74; question about 66; when to change 66-71. *See also* Reading faster

Reading versatility: developing 66-71

Reading vocabulary: *see* Vocabulary

Reasons: *explain* test question asking for 41; *how* test question asking for 43; paragraph patterns include 18; *why* test question asking for 42

Recalling: *see* Remembering

Recitations: tricks help prepare for 37-38. *See also* Self-quizzes

Reciting: *see* Recitations

Recognizing words: *see* Word recognition

Recreation: affects test preparation 33; making time for 72

Reference words: *see* Substitute words

Regressions: affect reading speed 72

Regular exceptions to vowel sound clues: *see* Vowel sound clues

Relating: *see* Connecting (relating) mentally

Relationships: appearance and sound of words 61-62, 64-65, 184-185, 186; ideas with whole lesson 24-25, 28-29; main ideas 21, 22, 24, 25-26, 27, 28, 28-29, 55, 78; main ideas and information 15, 21-22, 24-25, 27, 28, 28-29, 55, 58, 62; parts of lesson 19-23, 24, 24-25, 28-29, 78; parts of sentence 50-52; thoughts 54-55; time 50, 59; understanding 24-25, 27, 28, 28-29, 36, 53, 55-56, 62, 78; words in sentence 13-14, 49-50, 53. *See also* Ideas; Information

Relaxed, being: before tests 35; during tests 39, 40; needed for success 11

Remembering: curiosity and interest help 26, 28-29, 36; helping oneself strengthens 57; helps determine amount to read before self-quiz (reciting) 29, 56; lesson organization knowledge helps 19, 24-25, 28-29; organizing ideas and information helps 15, 16-17, 24-25, 28, 28-29, 30, 32, 36, 55-56, 108; previewing lesson helps 24-25, 28-29, 52-53; questioning helps 25-26, 27, 29, 52-53; reading speed and 68-70; relationship understanding helps 24-25, 28, 28-29, 36, 55-56; reviewing helps 27, 28, 30, 32, 56; selective 15, 60; self-quiz (reciting) helps 27, 29-30, 55-56; study skills knowledge helps 16, 16-17; suggestions for helping 33-34, 34, 36-38; test grade indicates 32; test preparation helps 32; thinking helps 36, 69. *See also* Comprehension; Forgetting; Ideas; Information; Understanding

Reports: finding information for 85-89; sources of information for 85-86

Rereading reviews: *see* Reviewing

Restrooms: using, before tests 34-35

Retelling reviews: *see* Reviewing

Review Words Notebook: using 65

Reviewing: rereading 17, 18, 27, 28, 30, 33, 56; retelling 28, 30, 33. *See also* Tests, getting ready for

Roman influence on other countries 161

Root words: *see* Roots

Roots: accent changes of, caused by suffix 170, 176-177; changing letters in 159-160, 170, 176; definition of 140; example of 140; fused with beginning of suffix 170, 176; Greek 161, 164-166; Latin 161-164, 164; meaning of, changed by prefixes 140-149; meaning of, changed by suffixes 140, 149-158; need for studying English 161; syllable division and 169; vowel-consonant teams in last syllable of 96, 97-98, 98, 118, 120, 123-124, 126, 126-128, 129-130, 132. *See also* Word meaning; Word recognition; Words

Saving time: finding answers for questions 80-84; finding information for reports 85-89; increasing reading speed helps 72; library use 86-87; prefix and suffix knowledge helps 140; Review Words Notebook helps 65; reviewing for tests 33; skill development practice helps 15-16, 75-76, 186; skimming helps 75, 78-79, 80-84, 85-89; studying lessons 16, 16-17, 26, 28-29, 72, 75, 78-79; Test Reminders Paper helps 33; tests and 39, 40, 43, 44; word learning 63, 65, 135, 184, 186. *See also* Wasting time

Saying information aloud: remembering information helped by 36

Scanning: *see* Skimming

Scared, being: before tests 35; during tests 40

Secondary accent: *see* Accent

Sections of a lesson: finding answers for questions in 80-84; general (overall) picture of ideas and information in 26, 29; main idea of 21, 22, 25-26, 27, 28, 28-29, 29-30, 55-56, 62, 78, 79; organization of 19-21, 21, 22, 23, 29, 55-56; part of lesson organization 19-21, 22, 23, 24-25, 28-29, 78; reviewing for tests 33; studying 17-18, 24, 25-27, 28, 29-30, 55-56, 78-79; understanding better 24, 78

Seeing and thinking: reading speed influenced by 73, 74; tachistascope quickens 74; time needed for 69

Self-Quiz and Recite: *see* Self-quizzes

Self-quizzes: after reading 17, 17-18, 27, 28, 29-30, 55-56; how much to read before 29, 56

Senses, the five: *see* Sensory imagery

Sensory imagery: remembering information helped by using 36; using, while reading 53-54, 58

Sentence meaning: *completion* tests affected by 44-45; conjunctions affect 50-52; development of 13-14; grouping words to get 13-14, 53; illustrated 13-14; punctuation marks affect 48-49, 63; substitute words affect 49-50; understanding 14, 44-45, 49-52, 53, 58; word-by-word reading affects understanding of 14, 53; word meaning affects 48, 61, 62, 63-64. *See also* Word meaning; Word recognition; Words

Sentence-type trick: remembering information helped by using 37-38

Short vowel sounds: *see* Vowel sounds, short

Silent consonants: *see* Consonants

Silent reading: parts of body needed for 73

Silent vowels: *see* Vowels

Similes: example of 58

Skill development: requirements for success in 11, 12, 15-16, 30, 71-72, 75-76, 107, 161; saving time by 15-16, 75-76, 186. *See also* Practice, regular; Success; Suggestions; Using information

Skim-Preview: *see* Lessons

Skimming: clue words used to help 80-81, 81, 82-83, 83; developing skill of 75-76; meaning of 75; mechanical devices for 74; scanning 75; studying helped by 17, 19, 24-25, 28, 28-29, 43, 52-53, 75, 75-76, 78-84, 85, 86-89; thinking while 24, 75, 78, 81, 82-83, 83, 87, 88; uses for, discussed 75

Sleep: affects test preparation 33

Slow reading: *see* Reading carefully; Study-type reading

Sounding out words: *see* Word recognition

Sounds: hearing of some, influenced by training 110, 122-123, 123, 124, 125; like *uh* 100, 185. *See also* Compound words; Consonants; Vowels; Words

Sources of information: for reports 85-86

Special cases: *ar* 118-119, 132; *er*, *ir*, *ur* 121-123, 132; *or* 124-126, 132

Speed lessons: using 73

Study schedule: using, for test preparation 33

Study skills: importance of 16, 16-17, 17-18. *See also* Study system; Study-type reading

Study system: discussed 24-30; need for using regularly 30

Study-type reading: amount of, before self-quiz (reciting) 29, 56; content area teachers and improvement of 57; dictionary used during 17, 62-63; finding answers for questions uses 81-82, 83; finding information for reports uses 87-88, 88-89, 89; getting ready for 17, 19, 22, 24-26, 28, 28-29, 52-53, 78-79, 80; improving 48-60; lessons 16, 16-17, 17-18, 19, 24-25, 25-27, 28, 29, 52, 53-57, 69, 70, 72, 80; paragraphs 15-18, 27, 29, 55-56, 62; skimming helps 17, 19, 24-25, 28, 28-29, 52-53, 75, 78-79, 80; teacher's thought-guiding questions for 80; transfer of learning 57; vocabulary-building helped by 64. *See also* Comprehension; Reading carefully; Understanding

Substitute words: discussed 49, 50; examples of 49-50

Subtitles: finding answers for questions uses 81, 82-83; lesson organization includes 19-21, 21, 22, 23, 24, 78; paragraphs before first of 22; purposes of 21, 22, 23, 24, 25-26, 27, 29, 33, 78, 81; reviewing for tests uses 33; study of lesson uses 24, 25-26, 27, 29, 52, 53, 78; subdivided sections 23

Success: key to 11, 32; school 43. *See also* Skill development

Suffixes: accenting 181; *ed* 97, 140, 149, 167-168; examples of 140, 149-158; fitting meaning of, to different words 152; fused with last letter of roots 170, 176; Greek roots with 164-165; importance of 140; introduction to examples of 141-142; Latin roots with 161-162, 163; list of many 150-158; meaning of 140; syllable division and 169, 170, 173; understanding of, needed 161. *See also* Roots; Word meaning; Word recognition

Suggestions: need for using 12, 71-72, 72-73, 186. *See also* Practice, regular; Skill development; Using information

Summary of lesson 23

Surveying lessons 17, 19, 24-25, 28, 28-29, 52-53, 78-79, 80. *See also* Skimming

Syllables: *ed* suffix 167-168; meaning of 167; number of, in a word 167-168, 170; sounding out 100, 169, 185-186

Syllables, accented: changes in 170, 175-177; meaning of 174. *See also* Vowels in accented syllables

Syllables, accenting: accent marks 174-175, 183; accent patterns 177-178, 178-179, 181; changes in accented syllable 170, 175-177; clues for 177, 178-183, change in 176-177, used with accent pattern information 177, 178-179; importance of 170, 174, 175-177; listening for 177; prefixes and 183; primary accent 175, 181-182, 183; reasons for 174, 176; recognized words 174; secondary accent 175, 181-182, 183; suffixes and 181; thinking 174; which syllable to accent 177-183. *See also* Word meaning; Word recognition

Syllables, dividing words into: clues for 170-173; number of syllables in a word 167-168, 170; things to do before 169-170; vowels divided 115

Syllables, unaccented: meaning of 174. *See also* Vowels in unaccented syllables

Table of contents: using 75, 83-84, 87, 88

Tables: *see* Illustrations

Tachistascopes: using 74

Talking about information: remembering information helped by 36

Teachers: need to stress suggestions 57; thought-guiding questions of 80

Teams: *see* Consonant teams; Vowel sound teams and vowel-consonant teams

Tense, being: before tests 35; need to stop 11

Tense of verb: changed by suffix 140, 149, 150

Term papers: *see* Reports

Test grades: discussed 32

Test Reminders Paper: using 33-34, 34, 36

Tests: meaning of, in this book 32

Tests, getting ready for: purpose of 32; suggestions for 32, 33-38; when to start 33

Tests, taking: directions for 39, 47; essay tests 39-44; forgetting 39-40, 43, 44, 45-46; general suggestions for 39; meaning of word *question* 44, 46; objective tests 44-47, examples of 46-47; organizing answers 39-40, 40; purpose of 32; suggestions for 32, 39-47

Things to remember: selecting 15, 60. *See also* Remembering

Thinking: critically 60; quickening 74; reading stopped for 69; remembering information helped by 36

Thinking and seeing: *see* Seeing and thinking

Thoughts: relating (connecting) new with familiar 54-55, 60

Throat muscle movements: affect reading speed 72

Time: conjunctions showing relationship of 50; *ed* suffix affects 140, 149, 150; vowel sounds and 131, 174. *See also* Saving time; Wasting time

Timed reading: using 73

Tongue movements: breaking habit 72; reading speed affected by 72

Topic sentence of paragraph 15, 16

Topics: finding — in card catalog 86-87, 88, in index 87, 88, in *Readers' Guide to Periodical Literature* 89, in table of contents 87, 88; finding information about, for reports 85-89

Transfer of learning: from reading class to other classes 57

Tricks: reading speed and 72-73; remembering information helped by using 37-38

Uh sounds: improper use of 100, 185

Unaccented syllables: *see* Syllables, unaccented

Understanding: curiosity and interest help 26; improving reading 48-60; lack of 56-57, 65, 66; prefixes help 140; reading speed and 66-71, 72, 73, 74; remembering information helped by 36; suffixes help 140; tachistascope quickens 74; using information helps 107; vocabulary affects 48, 58, 61, 62-63, 63-64, 67; what teachers emphasize 34. *See*

196

also Comprehension

Unfamiliar reading materials: *see* Reading materials

United States Government Printing Office: source of information for reports 85-86

Using information: remembering helped by 36; understanding helped by 107

Versatile reader: developing ability to be 66-71

Visualizing: hard-to-remember information 36; while reading 53-54, 58

Vivid reading 53-54

Vocabulary: development of 61-65; getting help from another person 56-57, 65; kinds of 61; meaning of 61; need for increasing 61; reading speed affected by 67, 73; saving time when building 63, 65, 135, 184, 186; suggestions for building 61-65. *See also* Word meaning; Word recognition; Words

Vowel-consonant teams: *see* Vowel sound teams and vowel-consonant teams

Vowel sound clues: exceptions to 107-108, 135-137; long 111-112; part of vowel sound study organization 108; purpose of 107-108; reasons for not working 117, 131, 174; regular exceptions to 108, 114-116, 117, 127, 127-128, 131; short 113

Vowel sound problem: discussed 107-109

Vowel sound teams and vowel-consonant teams: illustrated 117-130, 133, 134, 170; illustrating a use of *w* 105; illustrating *ch* sound for *t* 98; illustrating *sh* sound for *c* 96; illustrating *sh* sound for *t* 98; illustrating sounds for *s* 97-98; importance of 117; major teams 117-128; meaning of 117; minor teams 128-130; number of vowel sounds in 167; part of vowel sound study organization 108; sound of, borrowed by other letters 135, 136, 137; special cases of *ar* 118-119, 132; special cases of *er, ir, ur* 121-123, 132; special cases of *or* 124-126, 132; type of exception to vowel sound clues 108. *See also*

Roots

Vowel sounds, long: clues for using 111-112; examples of 111, 131, 133, 134; Freaks have 135, 136, 137; meaning of 111; part of vowel sound study organization 108; regular exceptions to vowel sound clues have 114, 115, 116; vowel team replacing 117

Vowel sounds, short: clue for using 113; examples of 113, 131, 133, 134; Freaks have 135, 136; part of vowel sound study organization 108; regular exceptions to vowel sound clues have 114, 114-115, 115-116; vowel team replacing 117

Vowel *y*: explained 110; listed 93

Vowels: confidence gained in using 107; dividing between 115; *i* using consonant *y* sound 133, 136-137; introduction to 107-109; learning about, discussed 107-109; list of 93; organizing study of 108; practice needed to understand 107; problem of 107-109; responsibility for learning about 107; silent 111, 112, 114-115, 115, 135, 136, 159, 160, 167, 185; sounds of 106-134, 185; summary of sounds 133-134; understanding, discussed 107-109; using borrowed sounds 133, 135, 136, 137. *See also* Freaks; Vowel sound clues; Vowel sound teams and vowel-consonant teams; Vowel sounds, long; Vowel sounds, short; Vowel *y*

Vowels in accented syllables: discussed 131, 132

Vowels in unaccented syllables: discussed 131-132; part of vowel sound study organization 108; reasons for special sound for many 131, 174; sounds of 131-132; special sound for many 131-132, 134; teams 132; type of exception to vowel sound clues 108; *y* 110

Warm-up, mental: before starting to read 52-53, 78

Wasting time: finding answers for questions 80; reading 72, 73; reviewing helps prevent 28; self-quiz (reciting) helps prevent 27; study skills knowledge helps prevent 16, 16-17; studying 33; words 65. *See also* Saving time

Who, what, when, where, why, how, how much, how many: questioning before reading uses 26, 29, 52; self-quiz (reciting) uses 55-56; sentences tell 13-14; test questions use 42-43

Word analysis: *see* Word recognition

Word attack: *see* Word recognition

Word-by-word reading: reading speed affected by 72; understanding of sentence meaning affected by 14, 53

Word length: using, to help figure out unrecognized words 185

Word meaning: accent might affect 175-176; compound words 139; Greek roots affect 161, 164-166; Latin roots affect 161-164, 164; listening helps in learning 61-62; prefixes affect 64, 140, 140-149, 161, 162; reading speed affected by 66-67, 73; remembering 61-62, 64-65; roots affect 64, 161; sentence meaning affects 50, 61-62, 63, 64, 65, 162; sentence meaning used to check 186; suffixes affect 64, 140, 149-158, 161, 162, 163; thinking about 53, 61-62, 64-65, 65, 80-81, 81, 82-83, 83. *See also* Sentence meaning; Vocabulary; Words

Word pictures: included in test answers 41

Word recognition: compound word knowledge helps 169; endings affect 159; example of word attack methods being used 17; figuring out unrecognized words 17, 61-62, 62, 67, 102, 107, 114, 117, 135, 140, 174, 184-186; Freaks 135; Greek root knowledge helps 164; knowing and using word attack suggestions 186; Latin root knowledge helps 162; listening helps 61-62; pausing between letters 100, 185; prefix knowledge helps 140, 162, 169; reading speed affected by 66-67, 73; regular exceptions to vowel sound clues 114; relatedness of appearance and sound of words 61-62, 64-65, 184-185, 186; root change knowledge helps 159; root knowledge helps 140; sentence meaning used to check correctness of fig-ured out word 186; sound clues and sentence meaning used together when figuring out unrecognized words 17, 184; sounding out words 17, 62, 100, 121-122, 125, 135, 169, 172, 174, 184-186; stopping between letters 100, 185; suffix knowledge helps 140, 159, 162, 169; team knowledge helps 102, 117; word analysis methods 184-186; word attack methods 184-186. *See also* Vocabulary; Words

Word shape: using, to help figure out unrecognized words 185

Word study charts: using 64

Word study information: using 64

Words: catchy 37; fixing in mind 61-62, 64-65, 117, 135, 186; forgetting 65; grouping, to get sentence meaning 13-14, 53; importance of using 65; listening to 61-62, 177; looks (appearance) of 61-62, 64-65, 135, 159, 184-185, 186; needed to express ideas and knowledge 164; reading speed affected by 66-67, 73; remembering 61-62, 64-65, 117, 135, 186; sound of, related to appearance of 61-62, 64-65, 184-185, 186; sounds of 17, 61-62, 62, 63-64, 64-65, 65, 135, 139, 174, 184-185, 186; thinking about 53, 61-62, 64-65, 65, 80-81, 81, 82-83, 83, 135, 186; understanding 58, 61, 140, 161; use of, in sentences 13-14, 17, 49-52, 53, 61-62, 62, 63, 64, 65, 162, 184, 186; using book's or magazine's exact 82, 83, 87-88, 89; with two or more meanings 64, 65, 175-176. *See also* Freaks; Roots; Vocabulary; Word meaning; Word recognition

Words, likenesses of: using, to help figure out unrecognized words 184-185

Working hard: needed for success 11

Worried, being: before tests 35; during tests 40; need to stop 11

Writing information: remembering information helped by 36

Y: *see* Consonant *y*; Vowel *y*